What Grievers Need:
God in the Midst of Stories of Comfort

Diane Pearson has empathetic ears, a caring heart, and open arms for those who seek comfort. She is a writer who ministers to hurting people through her stories, her lessons, and her prayers. This book provides balm and friendship to the downhearted. Open its pages and find restoration.
    Dr. Dennis E. Hensley, director of professional writing major at Taylor University and author of more than fifty books

Gifted author, Diane Pearson, has turned the God-affirming experiences of grieving people into meaningful devotions with the power to help and heal. Readers will encounter the God of all comfort as they read these inspiring accounts.
    Marcia Hornok, Managing Editor of *CHERA Fellowship*, a magazine for widows and widowers

The best description for this book is a healing touch with God at the center. I liked the individual, short stories that can be read a few at a time. This book would definitely be helpful to the grieving.
    Joyce, member of Compassionate Friends, a grief support group for those whose children have died. Her only child died at age twenty-one

Tears of thankfulness welled up as I read your words about our daughter, Bri. Thanks for sharing her passion for the Lord so beautifully and honoring her servant heart! We love knowing her story goes on and on. Thanks for the gift of your words in comforting others!
    Mary Kay and **Dan Esswein** of Long Beach, CA, whose twenty-five-year-old daughter died on the mission field in Nigeria

Diane has collected powerful, personal stories of God's grace in the midst of grief. My dad died in November, and even though I've written two books on death, Diane's book provided a wonderful comfort that went well beyond my academic research on the subject. I would highly recommend it.

James N. Watkins, author of the award-winning books *Death & Beyond* and *Is There Really Life After Death?* As an "ordained journalist," he has ministered for thirty-five years to those dying and those left behind.

This is a beautiful collection of stories and scriptures that will provide comfort and healing to those experiencing loss. It's helpful to draw upon others' experiences when going through a loss, as it lessens the feelings of isolation and provides much needed hope.

Lori, mental health RN who works with patients and families of the dying

GOD IN THE MIDST OF GRIEF

101 TRUE STORIES OF COMFORT

DIANE C. PEARSON

Carpenter's Son Publishing

God in the Midst of Grief: 101 True Stories of Comfort

Copyright © 2011 by Diane C. Pearson

All rights reserved. No part of this book may be reproduced or transmitted in any form or by any means, electronic or mechanical, including photocopying, recording or by any information storage and retrieval system, without permission in writing from the copyright owner.

Unless otherwise noted, Scripture references are taken from *The Holy Bible: New International Version* by Biblica. All other references are taken from T*he Holy Bible: King James Version*, as noted.

Published by Carpenter's Son Publishing, Franklin, Tennessee

Published in association with Larry Carpenter of Christian Book Services, LLC
www.christianbookservices.com

Printed in the United States of America

978-0-989849771-9-2

All rights reserved.

CONTENTS

Introduction —9—

Section One: God Prepares Our Hearts —11—
1. An Angel Named Joyce
2. The Holy Spirit Will Teach You All Things
3. Precious in the Sight of the Lord
4. When God Says: "Put Your House in Order"
5. Hallelujah Anyhow!
6. "I Am Not Going to Live a Long Life"
7. A Final Family Reunion

Section Two: God Provides —27—
8. In All Things God Works for Good
9. God Provides What We Need
10. God's Perfect Timing
11. God Can Cancel Our Reservations
12. God's Hand in the Details of Life
13. With God, There Are No Coincidences
14. The Miracle of Reconciliation
15. The Gift of Tears

Section Three: Unexpected Gifts —45—
16. Recover a Sense of Wonder about God
17. Detours Can Turn into Blessings
18. The Perfect Gift
19. Wind beneath My Wings
20. Foretaste of Heaven
21. A Father's Day Gift

Section Four: Signs of Comfort —61—
22. A Mother's Prayer for a Sign
23. The Miracle of the Rosebuds
24. Give God the Credit for Miraculous Signs
25. The Miracle of the White Dove
26. He Comforts Us in Our Troubles

Section Five: Miracles of Nature —73—
27. A Sign of God's Faithfulness
28. A Sweet Sign of Remembrance
29. God Answers Out of the Whirlwind
30. God Comforts on Special Days
31. A Rainbow Straight from Heaven
32. Memorial Day Remembrance
33. Butterflies: A Symbol of New Life
34. Lilacs and Lilies

Section Six: Angels Are Ministering Spirits —91—
35. Message for a Grieving Child
36. Guardian Angel Brings Strength and Comfort
37. Angelic Pallbearers
38. Angels Minister to the Dying
39. Angels in the Midst of Tragedy
40. Angels: God's Secret Agents
41. The Music Box Angels

Section Seven: Parting Gifts —111—
42. On This Side of Heaven's Door
43. Final Gifts: Communications of the Dying
44. A Child's Faith and Grandma's Last Goodbye
45. Heaven through a Mother's Eyes
46. The Last Supper
47. A Time to Mourn and a Time to Dance
48. "It's Just a Little Farther . . . It's Beautiful"
49. A Great Reunion in Heaven

Section Eight: Ready for Heaven —131—
  50. The Greeter
  51. In My Father's House Are Many Rooms
  52. I Know What Awaits Me
  53. Don't Worry About Me
  54. Are You Homesick for Heaven?
  55. What Will It Be Like When I Die?
  56. I'm Not Afraid to Die

Section Nine: Called to Comfort Others —147—
  57. Pray To Be Used and Then Obey
  58. One Small Act of Kindness
  59. God is Faithful When We Obey
  60. Called to Be Part of God's Buddy System
  61. Show Each Other Your Wounds
  62. We Are Bound Together by Jesus Christ

Section Ten: Called to Witness —161—
  63. A Joyful Witness for Christ
  64. The Privilege of Witnessing for Christ
  65. The Miracle of Salvation
  66. Always Be Prepared to Share the Good News
  67. Never Too Old to Witness
  68. Say "I Love You" Before It's Too Late
  69. A Second Chance to Love My Father

Section Eleven: Grief at the Holidays —179—
  70. Are Christians Allowed to Be Depressed?
  71. Giving Thanks, Even in Grief
  72. Gift of Comfort at the Holidays
  73. First Christmas in Heaven
  74. Will Your Passing Leave a Hole in the World?
  75. If This New Year's Eve Were Your Last

Section Twelve: Precious Memories   —195—
   76. Cleaning Out the House
   77. In Remembrance of a Soldier
   78. He Raced into the Arms of Jesus
   79. A Life that Matters
   80. You Won't Be Crippled in Heaven

Section Thirteen: Why, God?   —209—
   81. When We Do Not Understand
   82. No One Is Exempt
   83. Trust the Lord with All Your Heart
   84. Are You Stuck in Grief?
   85. Let Go of Your Anger
   86. Run the Race Set before You
   87. Looking for Jesus
   88. The Mystery of It All

Section Fourteen: Growth through Grief   —229—
   89. From Wailing to Singing
   90. Lean on a Solid Foundation
   91. Give Your Grief to the Lord
   92. Ask for a Double Portion
   93. With God's Help You Can Go On
   94. Unexpected Signs of Life

Section Fifteen: Joy in the Midst of Grief   —245—
   95. Can You Choose to Be Joyful?
   96. The Gift of Baby Andrew
   97. A Time to Be Born and a Time to Die
   98. The Heroes of the Faith among Us
   99. Because He Lives
   100. Turn to Him and Embrace the Promise
   101. Such a Simple Message: Choose Joy

INTRODUCTION

God in the Midst of Grief: 101 True Stories of Comfort is a collection of newspaper columns I wrote over a period of ten years (1999 to 2009). My weekly column for the religion page of *The Times* in Frankfort, Indiana, was titled, "Real-Life Devotions," true stories of God working in people's lives.

When readers asked for books of my stories, I organized them into different topics. A powerful theme emerged: more than a hundred of the five hundred stories related to grief and sorrow in some way, universal emotions we all experience at some point in our lives.

The longer I wrote my column, the more I heard from readers: "I had a similar experience when my loved one died. Will you write my story?" Or, "I've never told anyone this story before, but I want people to hear it."

Many of these stories are miraculous—angel encounters, visions, and signs that the loved one is in heaven. Others are testimonies to God's faithfulness during times of grief—how God prepares our hearts for the death of a loved one, how he sends the perfect people alongside us, and how he orchestrates miracles of his perfect timing.

Still others deal with grief at the holidays, birthdays, or anniversaries and how God comforts us on those special days.

The chapter "Why, God?" shows that Christians are allowed to question God, especially in unexpected or tragic deaths that we do not understand. Readers draw strength from stories of how other people coped. We may not receive answers until we get to heaven, but we can be assured that God grieves with us, he hears our anger and pain, and he will always be there to help us walk through the trials.

Finally, I share stories of people looking back at times of grief, how they grew through the experience, and how they can comfort and witness to others.

One of the main purposes of this book is to show that ordinary people—like you and me—can experience God in powerful and miraculous ways, especially during times of suffering. The hope is that by reading about other people's God experiences, your eyes will be opened to God working in your own life.

The material in this book will appeal to people at any stage or age of life. Let's face it. The statistics on physical death are quite clear: one out of one of us will die. You will experience loss, whether it's parents or grandparents after a long, full life, or babies who never took their first breath.

These stories do not focus on the sadness and pain of physical death, but on the God-given promises of heaven and eternal life. Each story is based on Scripture and ends with a prayer pointing people to Jesus Christ.

In a few of the stories, people asked me to change their names because of the intensely personal nature of their experiences. I always honored their wishes.

I put the words to paper, but I am merely a conduit for God's work as he nudged people to share their stories with me. It is my privilege to pass them on to you.

Diane Pearson

Note: Also available with this book:
Companion Guide for God in the Midst of Grief
Questions for group discussion or
personal reflection with space for journaling.

SECTION ONE

GOD PREPARES OUR HEARTS

1

An Angel Named Joyce

I am sending an angel ahead of you to guard you along the way and to bring you to the place I have prepared.

EXODUS 23:20

Her name was Joyce. We were never allowed to know her last name or her address. Maybe angels don't have last names or addresses. All I know is that Joyce appeared in my father's life at precisely the right time to usher him peacefully into the presence of God, and, like all good angels, she disappeared when her job was completed.

My dad was dying from congestive heart failure. Joyce was a home health care nurse who visited him every day for the last few weeks of his life. This was my first experience with the dying process. I never knew the right words to say, but Joyce always had the right words. She let him talk when he needed to talk and cry when he needed to cry. It seems that people outside the family have a greater freedom to talk to the terminally ill. Maybe that's why God uses them so effectively. Joyce wasn't afraid to broach the subject of death.

"You know you're going to die from this, don't you?" Joyce asked.

Dad cried and said, "Yes, but I don't want to go back to the hospital again."

"Are you trying to tell me you want to die at home?"

Yes, I want to die at home," he said.

"We can arrange that," Joyce assured him.

Not only did Joyce arrange for his physical care, but she also undertook his spiritual care. Every day she planted a different seed of thought, gently moving him closer to his heavenly home.

"Do you believe in God?" she asked one day. "You need to say your prayers and get right with God."

"I'm right with God," he assured her.

Another day she asked, "Is there anyone you need to make peace with before you die?" She knew that sometimes people linger because of unresolved conflicts.

Perhaps the most helpful thing Joyce said to him was, "Don't be afraid."

Saying those words must be part of the job description for angels because they were used in the Bible frequently. In Luke 1:30 an angel appeared to Mary to inform her she was with child, saying, "Do not be afraid." An angel said to Joseph in Matthew 1:20, "Do not be afraid to take Mary as your wife." And in Acts 27:24 an angel appeared to Paul after he was shipwrecked, saying, "Do not be afraid, Paul."

God promised the Israelites in Exodus 23:20, "I am sending an angel ahead of you to guard you along the way and to bring you to the place I have prepared."

Joyce was the angel who prepared the way for my father to face death unafraid. He died at home in his own bed completely at peace with God and with himself.

Dear Heavenly Father, thank you for angels like Joyce who minister to us at exactly the right moments with exactly the right words. Help us remember that we are your hands and feet, commissioned to carry out your work here on earth. In the name of Jesus Christ we pray. Amen.

2

The Holy Spirit Will Teach You All Things

"The Holy Spirit, whom the Father will send in my name, will teach you all things."

JOHN 14:26

I went to a funeral visitation for a woman named Evelyn, who fought a long battle against cancer. I spoke with one of her daughters in the receiving line who said, "Mom was diagnosed with terminal cancer seven years ago. Doctors said she would die within six months to one year, but Mom knew better. She said, 'I know what the doctors are saying, but I just don't feel like it's my time.'"

Evelyn was right. God spoke to her Spirit and told her it was not her time to die, and she refused to live like someone with a death sentence. She was an active, contributing member of society for seven years and a blessing to those around her. You can be given a death sentence by earthly doctors, but the Great Physician may have other plans.

About one month before Evelyn died, her son came to visit from Texas. "I'm glad you came," she said. "It's almost my time. I'm going to die in a month."

Evelyn died one month and two days later.

How did God speak to Evelyn like this? The same way he speaks to all believers: through the power of the Holy Spirit living inside us. Jesus promised the disciples that, when he returned to heaven, the Holy Spirit would come in his place (John 16:7). As believers, we have that same Holy Spirit living in us. The Holy Spirit is God himself, residing in our bodies, guiding and directing us.

Yes, the Holy Spirit can communicate to us that our earthly death is imminent, just as he did with Evelyn. But, just as surely, he can assure us that earthly death is the beginning of eternal life with him.

Dear Heavenly Father, thank you that you can prepare our hearts for the end of our physical bodies and the beginning of our heavenly bodies. In the name of Jesus Christ we pray. Amen.

3

Precious in the Sight of the Lord

All Scripture is God-breathed and is useful for teaching, rebuking, correcting and training in righteousness.

2 TIMOTHY 3:16

"God speaks to us through the Word of God, the Bible," said the teacher. Our church was doing a video study called *The Alpha Course*[1] based on a book by Nicky Gumbel, *Questions of Life: A Practical Introduction to the Christian Faith*.[2]

"Let me tell you how God spoke to me in a very specific way ten days after my father's death," said Gumbel. "I was worried that my father had not accepted Christ before he died. I asked God to speak to me about that."

He said, "I happened to be reading Romans when I came across the verse, 'Everyone who calls on the name of the Lord will be saved' (Romans 10:13). I sensed at that moment God was saying to me that this verse was for my father, that he had called on the name of the Lord before he died."

Five minutes later Gumbel's wife came in and said, "I'm reading Acts. I think this verse is for your father: 'Everyone who calls on the name of the Lord will be saved' (Acts 2:21)."

"It was quite extraordinary," said Gumbel, "because that verse only appears twice in the New Testament. God spoke to both of us through the same words at the same time in different parts of the Bible."

God's confirmation didn't end there. Three days later, he went to a Bible study in a friend's home. The study was on Romans 10:13, the same verse. Then, to top it off, the next day he came out of the subway station in London and looked up at a huge poster that said, "Everyone who calls upon the name of the Lord will be saved. Romans 10:13."

In our class discussion following the video, one of the students named Wanda said, "I know Scripture can speak to people like that. When my mother was in the final stages of cancer, I had a difficult time letting go of her. The family took turns reading to her from the Bible. I was reading Psalm 116. When I got to verse 15, I felt the Lord speak to me in these words: 'Precious in the sight of the Lord is the death of his saints.'"

Later that day Wanda picked up her daily devotional book. The Scripture for the day was Psalm 116:15, "Precious in the sight of the Lord is the death of his saints."

"I knew God was preparing my heart for my mother's death. She died later that day."

God added one last touch of comfort. When Wanda returned home at 11 o'clock that night, she found a card on her kitchen table from a neighbor. It was signed, "This verse seemed appropriate: Psalm 116:15, 'Precious in the sight of the Lord is the death of his saints.'"

Dear Heavenly Father, thank you for your loving kindness toward us through the death of a loved one. You prepare us and comfort us with your Word. Thank you for being the Great Comforter. In the name of Jesus Christ we pray. Amen.

---

1. The Alpha Course (London: Alpha International, 1995).

2. Gumbel, Nicky. *Questions of Life: A Practical Introduction to the Christian Faith.* (Colorado Springs: Cook Communications Ministries, 1993), 81-82.

4

When God Says: Put Your House in Order

"This is what the Lord says: 'Put your house in order, because you are going to die.'"

2 KINGS 20:1

We all know people, perhaps family, who were told by their doctors, "Put your house in order," code words for, "Make preparations because you don't have long to live."

But do you know people who were given this same message—put your house in order—not from human lips, but from God?

A young man named Lee from Goshen, Indiana, was raised in the church, and christened by his uncle, Rev. Ira Crise. "Lee was dedicated to the Lord as an infant," said Rev. Crise. "God had his hand on him from the beginning."

Lee was in the Army for ten years, a career soldier who saw a lot of action. His third baby was born after he was sent back to Iraq. He got a leave to come home at Thanksgiving to see the new baby.

Many people in the family said Lee was different when he came home. He had a premonition about his death and spoke openly about it. In fact, he talked to Rev. Crise about funeral arrangements and chose the cemetery where he wanted to be buried.

"I wasn't the only one he expressed these feelings to," said Rev. Crise. "My sister [Lee's grandmother] also said Lee made sure all his business affairs were in order. He told his wife and mother, 'If anything should happen to me, this is what I want done.' He told them both he might not be back."

At a family get-together on November 15, Lee asked for prayer. They gathered around him and laid hands on Lee, as he recommitted his heart and life to the Lord. Lee was amazed at what he felt—the presence of the Lord. After that, he had a peace and calm that never left him.

Rev. Crise said, "I remember the date because December 5 is my birthday. We were having a birthday celebration at my church when we got the news that Lee had been killed while on patrol in Iraq. He'd been hit by an IED [improvised explosive device] and died instantly. Lee was only 28 and the father of three small children.

"But Lee definitely had his house in order. He not only expected and planned for his physical death, but he was ready to go spiritually. Without a doubt, Lee is with the Lord."

George Bernard Shaw said: "The statistics on death are quite impressive. One out of one people die."

Why is it, then, that so few of us prepare for death? We all have the opportunity to put our spiritual house in order by accepting Jesus Christ as our Lord and Savior.

Dear Heavenly Father, guide us to surrender our hearts and our lives to you, and order our lives in such a way that we bring you all the glory and honor. In the name of Jesus Christ we pray. Amen.

5

Hallelujah Anyhow!

"I heard . . . a great multitude in heaven shouting: 'Hallelujah!'"
REVELATION 19:1

"My grandmother influenced my life more than I could ever have imagined," said Michele. "There was always a special connection between us. As I grew into a young woman, I sought her counsel often. She was completely rooted in the Word of God. She could find the answer to any question in the Bible. Gram's life motto was: 'Hallelujah anyhow!' She would often say, "If life's troubles come your way, just lift your head up high and say 'Hallelujah anyhow!'" Life dealt Gram many sorrows, but she overcame them all.

"In November 2003 I planned a 'girl's night out' with my mother and grandmother. My mother wasn't feeling well and didn't go with us, but I took Gram to see a musical. When I took her home, as usual, I watched her to see that she made it to the door and inside the house safely. As I watched her walk up the sidewalk, the Lord spoke to me audibly: 'This is the last outing you will have with her.'

"It gave me chills, but I knew without a doubt God had spoken to me. I praised and thanked him that we had shared such a special evening."

The next day Michele's grandmother experienced a lung hemorrhage. Within days, she was diagnosed with lung cancer.

"I spent three weeks in the hospital with her day and night, and then I moved her home with me. During the next six weeks, we shared many things about the Lord and about life. She told me I was born to take over where she would leave off. I witnessed in my spirit that she was telling me the truth.

"When the end drew near, Gram called out to me, 'Baby, do you see them?' She pointed toward the ceiling and called out the names of four children who predeceased her. 'They're coming for me,' she said, 'but not quite yet.'

"I told her to rest so she would be ready. That was the last conversation we had.

Within the hour, her soul departed her body. I have been in some spirit-filled worship services, but never experienced the powerful presence of God that I did at her death. I asked God to let me see her out of my arms and into his. He granted me just that. We serve a truly merciful God."

Dear Heavenly Father, thank you for this beautiful witness, in death as well as in life. We know she is in heaven shouting, "Hallelujah anyhow!" In the name of Jesus Christ we pray. Amen.

6

"I Am Not Going to Live a Long Life"

"Our end was near, our days were numbered."

LAMENTATIONS 4:18

After a young medical missionary named Brianna died at the age of 25 in Nigeria, various friends and acquaintances added their memories of her to her website. Dr. Cliff Kelly, one of Bri's teachers who helped prepare her for the mission field, said he was deeply grieved at the loss of so extraordinary a Christian woman. But he was not surprised. He wrote:

"She frequently dropped by my office to chat. One day I asked her questions about her love for Africa and whether or not she had ever thought about having a family someday.

"She answered, 'Dr. K, I won't ever have a family.'

"I was shocked by her firm but pleasant response and asked her why she knew this.

"'Because the Lord has made it clear to me. Dr. K, I am not going to live a long life.'

"My jaw must have dropped to the floor, but I immediately knew that she was telling me the truth of what our sweet Lord had somehow shared with her during her tender years. Why? To fully prepare her for the day she would go home to be with her Master. She knew she would perish on the mission field, for the glory of God and the fulfillment of her ministry to the hurting. It is he who decides our course when we are totally submitted to his perfect will."[1]

Brianna knew her life would be short. God in his wisdom revealed that to her and prepared her to meet him. Perhaps that is why she lived her life so passionately, knowing her time on earth was limited.

> *Dear Heavenly Father, it's a mystery to us how you can speak to our hearts and spirits as you did with Bri. But you know the course of each of our lives. Let us all follow her example and live our lives passionately for you. In the name of Jesus Christ we pray. Amen.*

---

1. Kelly, Cliff, Ph.D., entry on website: www.bethanylutheran.org/brimemories.html, Jan. 5, 2006, p. 21.

7

A Final Family Reunion

"Blessed are those who mourn, for they shall be comforted."

MATTHEW 5:4

Sunday morning, August 20, 2000, I was reading my daily devotional book. The lesson for that day was from Matthew 5:4, "Blessed are those who mourn, for they shall be comforted." That verse had special meaning for me because my dad was in the process of dying.

When you know a loved one is dying, the mourning process begins even before the death. I think it's God's way of preparing our hearts. I read the lesson to my husband, Lin. "I think God is preparing me for Dad's death," I said.

My devotional book is also a prayer journal. Exactly one year earlier, on August 20, 1999, my parents were visiting from Florida. I wrote these words in my prayer journal that day: "We had a wonderful day—a family reunion with Mom and Dad and all the relatives. Seventeen people were here for dinner. It's rare that we all get together. Dad is not doing very well. This may be the last family reunion we have before a funeral."

My dad suffered from heart problems for years. After his third open-heart surgery, the doctors didn't think he would survive. He surprised everyone by fighting back. He lived another three years, but he suffered a long, slow decline from congestive heart failure. He struggled to live; then he struggled to die. My prayer for him was that he would die in peace.

Later that morning in church, a girl named Jessica was scheduled to sing a solo. She prefaced her song with these comments: "I'm not going to sing the song listed in the bulletin. God has led me to sing a different song today, one that I composed myself. It's called 'Grant Me Peace.'"

I turned to Lin and said, "That's what I've been praying for Dad—that God would grant him peace."

As I closed my eyes and listened to the words of that song, I knew they were from God. I claimed those words for my father.

Dad passed away peacefully several hours later. He went on to his own family reunion with his mother, father, and others who had passed on before him. And I know he also had a glorious reunion with Jesus Christ. That family reunion in August, 1999, was, indeed, the last one with my dad. The rest of us prepared for another type of family reunion as we made funeral arrangements.

God prepared my heart in very tender ways. He comforted me before my father's death, and he comforted our family through the funeral process—a bittersweet family reunion.

Dear Heavenly Father, we all look forward to that great reunion in heaven with our loved ones and with your son Jesus Christ. It is in his name that we pray. Amen.

SECTION TWO

GOD PROVIDES

8

In All Things God Works for Good

And we know that in all things God works for the good of those who love him, who have been called according to his purpose.

ROMANS 8:28

Jim's eighty-eight-year-old mother, Esther, always lived in her own home, but after a stroke, that was impossible. She was transferred from the hospital to a nursing home.

Jim had recently lost his job, which turned out to be a blessing in disguise because he was able to visit her every day.

On a Sunday morning in January, Jim went to see her. From the intercom came this announcement: "The morning worship service will start in the lounge in ten minutes."

"Do you feel like going to the service?" asked Jim.

"Yes," she said, so he pushed her down the hall in a wheelchair.

As they sat there waiting for the service to begin, a woman approached Jim and asked, "You're a minister, aren't you?"

"Yes," he responded. (Do pastors have a special look about them?)

"Our regular minister is on vacation," she said, "and the substitute didn't show up. Could you possibly preach for us today?"

"Give me five extra minutes to collect my thoughts," said Jim, as he grabbed a Bible. He chose to preach on Romans 8:28, "And we know that in all things God works for the good of those who love him, who have been called according to his purpose."

"I intended for it to be a pep talk for my mom," he said, "that all things, even in the difficult circumstances of living in a nursing home after a stroke, work together for the good of those who love him."

That was the last sermon Esther ever heard. She went home to be with the Lord the following Saturday.

Jim said, "It was a genuine privilege to minister to my mother in that way. God arranged for the substitute pastor to be a 'no-show' so I could give that final gift to my mother."

The next morning Jim and his wife were doing their Bible study. The verse for that day was Romans 8:28! Jim's wife said, "It was affirmation to us that Jim's last sermon for his mother was the one the Lord wanted her to hear. It was God's perfect timing."

> *Dear Heavenly Father, thank you for Jim's response to give the last sermon for his mother. We always have a choice when you ask us to do something. Help us to be obedient, for through obedience we and others may be profoundly blessed. Thank you that all things work together for the good of those who love you. In the name of Jesus Christ we pray. Amen.*

9

God Provides What We Need

*He has sent me to bind up the brokenhearted . . . .
and provide for those who grieve.*

ISAIAH 61:1, 3

My twenty-six-year-old daughter, Shelley, was home from Seattle for Christmas. She has a very good friend named Michelle, whom she tries to visit when she's home. It used to be a threesome: Shelley, Michelle, and Erin. They became fast friends in high school when they attended church camp together, but Erin died in a motorcycle accident six months earlier.

Shelley and Michelle met for supper and talked about old times. Shelley had a picture of the three of them smiling, with arms intertwined. They framed a copy of it to give to Erin's parents for Christmas.

They decided to stop by a flower shop to get some flowers for Erin's grave. It was closing time, and things were already put away. The woman suggested roses, but Michelle asked, "Do you have any daisies?"

"We had some earlier, but I think I used them all. I'll check." She returned a few moments later with two stems of yellow daisies, each with several blooms. "I'm afraid this is all I have."

"That's perfect!" said Michelle. "Yellow was Erin's favorite color, and yellow daisies were her favorite flower."

They made their way to the cemetery and traipsed through the snow until they found Erin's grave. Shelley said a little prayer, thanking God for Erin's life and the people she touched, and then they each placed their yellow daisies on the grave.

This story reminded me of another woman named Karolyn, a young wife and mother, who died after a long battle with cancer. Lore, her best friend, knew that Calla lilies were Karolyn's favorite flowers.

Lore was so distraught over her friend's death that she forgot about buying flowers for the funeral until the morning of the service. When she went to a flower shop and asked for Calla lilies, the man said, "Calla lilies come from South America, and this is the wrong time of the year for them. You won't be able to find any."

Nevertheless, Lore went to another florist with the same request. The woman said, "I can't believe you're asking for Calla lilies. I just got some in this morning, but I had no idea what I was going to do with them. I didn't order them. No one had requested them."

Lore said, "They're for me. I'm supposed to buy those for my friend's funeral this morning."

Lore carried the flowers to the funeral home and placed them on a small table inside the front door. Later in the morning, she noticed that someone had moved the flowers next to Karolyn's wedding picture where she was holding Calla lilies.

God provided what was needed.

Dear Lord, thank you for the little acts of tenderness you show us when we are grieving. You provide exactly what we need when we need it. In the name of Jesus Christ we pray. Amen.

10

God's Perfect Timing

There is a time for everything, and a season for every activity under heaven.

ECCLESIASTES 3:1

"Dad's ninetieth birthday is next Wednesday," said Eleanor. "I'm planning to bring cake and ice cream for a surprise party. Could you have people down in the lounge around 6 PM?"

"Sure," said the nursing home staff. "We'll plan on it."

But on Wednesday morning, Eleanor looked at the calendar and made a crazy discovery: her dad's birthday was on Thursday. She had planned the party a day early!

In addition to the people at the nursing home, she had invited family and friends. Since the arrangements were already made, she decided to go ahead with the party.

"Dad was especially alert that day," said Eleanor. "He was blessed with a lot of visitors. He was very pleased, and everyone had a great time."

But God definitely had a plan for this "mistake" in dates. Eleanor's dad died peacefully later that night. Eleanor said, "If not for God's perfect timing, Dad would have missed his final birthday party."

How many times have we questioned the wisdom of God's timing, only to discover later that his ways are perfect?

As I prayed about this story, the Holy Spirit reminded me of Ecclesiastes 3:1-2, those beautiful verses about time that are so often recited at funerals: "There is a time for everything, and a season for every activity under heaven: a time to be born and a time to die."

I use a study Bible with questions in the margin. As if to confirm that I chose the right verse, the first study question for that passage was: "What is the most important date you ever forgot?"[1]

Perhaps we have all forgotten important dates, but we can be sure that God never forgets. He has a celebration planned for us in heaven far better than any party we could plan here on earth. Only he knows the exact date and time.

> *Dear Heavenly Father, thank you for this story of your perfect timing. When events do not proceed exactly as we want, help us to stop and pray. You may be working in a miraculous way that we do not see until events unfold. In the name of Jesus Christ we pray. Amen.*

---

1. *Serendipity Bible, 10th Anniversary Edition*, NIV (Grand Rapids: Zondervan Publishing House and Serendipity House, 1988), 933.

11

God Can Cancel Our Reservations

*Many are the plans in a man's heart,
but it is the Lord's purpose that prevails.*

PROVERBS 19:21

"What do you mean you're not going? We made reservations!"

"I just don't want to go!" said John.

Nancy and her husband, John, were having a disagreement about reservations with Nancy's mother for dinner and a program at the retirement home where she lived. Just when they were ready to walk out the door, John informed her he wasn't going.

"But, John, we made reservations and already paid for everything."

"I don't know why I don't want to go. I just don't want to go!"

Nancy was put out with him, but no amount of coaxing could get him to change his mind. Nancy went on by herself to meet her mother for dinner, a drive of more than an hour.

Dessert was being served when someone from the retirement home approached Nancy and said, "You need to call home right away."

When she got John on the phone, he said, "Your brother, Larry, has been taken by Lifeline to the hospital. He's unconscious and very critical. You and your mother need to get to Indianapolis right away."

Nancy returned to the dining room to get her mother. As they were walking out, obviously distraught, a friend asked what was wrong. Nancy explained the emergency and said, "I can't remember how to get to the hospital. Can you give me directions?"

The man said, "You're not going by yourself. I'll take you." It was an hour's drive.

Nancy said, "Mom and I made it down to the hospital that evening, but Larry never regained consciousness. He died a week later.

"I can see now how God worked in these events surrounding my brother's death. It all started with a disagreement with my husband! It was such a blessing that John was home to get that phone call and knew how to get in touch with me. God arranged for me to be with my mother when we got the distressing news, and he even arranged for a friend to drive us to the hospital. God was in control the whole time."

Dear Heavenly Father, thank you that you are especially close to us in times of crisis, working out the details of our lives, even when we are not aware of it, and even when our actions don't make sense to those around us. Remind us often that you see the whole tapestry of life. Help us to trust your guidance. In Jesus' name, Amen.

12

God's Hand in the Details of Life

*Grow in the grace and knowledge of
our Lord and Savior Jesus Christ.*

2 PETER 3:18

"As I grow in my Christian walk," said Carol, "I recognize God's hand more and more in my life."

Carol and her mother worked together doing alterations for a bridal shop. They consistently had two weeks of work lined up, so it was a mystery to them one February when all of a sudden the work stopped coming in.

Carol said to her husband, "It's strange that we don't have any work scheduled the first two weeks in February. I can't understand it."

Their business had always depended on word of mouth. That obviously wasn't working, so they decided to spend some money on advertising. Right before Carol went to the newspaper to run an ad, God showed her why her calendar was cleared: Carol's father died suddenly of a heart attack the first week of February.

Carol said, "It's easy to see in hindsight that God lovingly arranged the details of our work so that my mother and I could be free those two weeks. We didn't have to go through the hassle of rescheduling appointments. We were able to put a 'Closed' sign on the door and not worry about it. What a blessing!"

Business immediately went back to normal after the funeral.

Carol said, "I used to get upset when people cancelled appointments. Now instead of complaining about it, I ask myself: *Could God be working here?* The cancellation could be related to something in my life or God could be working in the life of the customer."

One of the most difficult things to learn in the Christian walk is that God longs to arrange the details of our lives if we will submit to his gentle guidance. He knows the future and his plans will prevail, with or without our cooperation. The creator of the universe wants to be in charge of our lives through the power of the Holy Spirit living inside all believers.

The next time your schedule is changed inexplicably, ask: "God, are you working here?" Then watch and wait for an answer.

Dear Heavenly Father, remind us often that you see the whole picture, every detail. Help us to trust your guidance, even when we don't understand. Help us to see your hand in our lives through the power of the Holy Spirit. In the name of Jesus Christ we pray.
Amen.

13

With God, There Are No Coincidences

The hand of the Lord has done this.

ISAIAH 41:20

I made a trip to an Indianapolis hospital where a friend of mine was having a very serious surgery. I sat in the waiting room with his wife, Nancy, and son, Kevin, for several hours.

Kevin had been commissioned into ministry six months earlier. His pastoral education included chaplaincy rotations in three different hospitals. His dad's surgery was in one of them, so Kevin was familiar with the workings of that hospital. Kevin spent some time that day visiting with friends in the chaplain's office.

Kevin and I got into a conversation about the chaplaincy program and what excellent training it is for ministry. Kevin said, "One of the most difficult situations is when you are called to be with a family who has made the decision to take a loved one off life support. I was sitting in the chaplain's office one day when a nurse called with just that situation. The protocol is that the staff chaplain is paged first. He was unavailable. The on-call chaplain is notified next. He, too, was unavailable, so I volunteered to go.

"I did a lot of praying on my way there. I walked into the patient's room and introduced myself to the family. A man stood at his father's bedside with his back to me, but even from the back, I thought he looked familiar. When he turned around to face me, I knew without a doubt God had arranged for me to be there.

"That man was the lawyer who had handled the adoption proceedings for our son, Spencer, four years earlier. He helped bring a new life into my family. Now I was ministering to him as his father was exiting life. There are no coincidences. This was a God incident."

Dear Heavenly Father, thank you for your guiding hand in our daily lives. May our eyes, ears and hearts always be open to your provision. Help us to respond the way you want us to respond. In the name of Jesus Christ we pray. Amen.

14

The Miracle of Reconciliation

We were reconciled to God through the death of his Son.

ROMANS 5:10

"Reconciliation" is a big word with a big meaning. Literally, it means "to bring things that have been separated together again." The greatest act of reconciliation in history was the death of Jesus on the cross. He took our sins upon himself so we could be reconciled with God.

But reconciliation also refers to our relationships with other people. Broken relationships can hinder our relationship with God. Can you look at the face of Christ and not forgive others?

Elaine had a troubled childhood with an alcoholic father and an emotionally remote mother. "I can't remember a time when my father was sober, and only twice in my life can I remember when my mother physically touched me. I ended up in a series of foster homes and spent most of my life very angry at them.

"But that all changed when both parents were diagnosed with terminal cancer within a week of each other. In spite of my anger, I knew God was calling me to reconcile with them before it was too late."

Elaine began nursing her mother first: injections four times a day; medicines to administer; twice-weekly doctor appointments. She spent weeks sleeping on the floor of her mother's bedroom in case she needed something during the night.

Elaine said, "I was privileged to hold my mother's hand and talk to her for four straight days before she died. It was such a blessing, as I got to know the woman who birthed me. This woman was no longer a cold stranger to me. More important, she accepted Jesus Christ as her Savior."

Elaine's journey of reconciliation did not end there. "My father began to fail rapidly soon after Mom died. He had no access to alcohol, so for the first time in my life I got to speak to and spend time with a sober father. What an answer to prayer! He turned out to be a pretty nice guy who had suffered with his own demons since childhood. I was able to hold his hand and pray for him as he passed from this life to the next. In that moment, I forgave everything he had ever done in my past. He became my dad."

When Elaine tries to explain to people how she was able to forgive, she says, "It was no longer about what kind of parents they had been to me. It was about what kind of daughter I could be to them. My prayers were answered, as I was able to forgive them and others, as he forgives me daily. By doing the hard work of forgiveness required of me by the Lord, I was open to receive the gifts my parents offered me at the end of their lives. They were able to lay down their shame and feel forgiveness. I will always be grateful."

They all experienced the miracle of reconciliation.

> *Dear Heavenly Father, thank you for giving us the means to reconcile with each other while there is still time. Search our hearts. Bring to mind those with whom you want us to reconcile. Provide us with the strength to forgive others as you forgive us. Thank you for the gift of your son Jesus Christ, whose death on the cross reconciled us to you. It is in his name we pray. Amen.*

15

The Gift of Tears

My intercessor is my friend as my eyes pour out tears to God.

JOB 16:20

Angela's four-year-old daughter loved to dance. She was always excited about the Wednesday night classes where she took lessons with older, more experienced girls. She progressed quickly, but the following year the teacher placed her in a class of beginners.

"I didn't understand that, so I talked to the teacher about it," said Angela. "She convinced me that sometimes it's not the skill level that makes a successful class, but the personalities of the children involved. I reluctantly went along with her decision."

The parents of the kids sat on the sidelines during class and developed friendships. Angela's minister, Pastor Lore, happened to be one of those parents at a time when Angela's father was terminally ill.

Two months into that class, Angela's dad passed away. She said, "I was so emotional after he died that it was impossible to sit through a church service without sobbing. I was embarrassed at the display of tears, so I quit attending church."

One Wednesday night Angela shared her struggle with Pastor Lore. "Don't stop coming to church," she said. "It's okay to cry. Sometimes when there are no more prayers left to be said, then your tears become a form of prayer."

Angela said, "I thought about Pastor Lore's words. I always felt that my most important job as a parent was to rear Christian children, so I followed her advice and went back to church for the sake of my kids, even though it was difficult to sit through a service."

Many changes occurred during the next four years. Pastor Lore was transferred to another church. Angela's oldest child, a fourteen-year-old son, completed confirmation classes, an intensive nine-month study of the Bible to prepare him to become a full-fledged member of the church.

Angela said, "We attended a confirmation banquet at the end of the class, followed by a moving service in the sanctuary. The confirmands received Communion from the pastor. In turn, each confirmand served Communion to his or her family. We all laid hands on our children and prayed for them.

"It was a very emotional service," said Angela. "All I could do was cry. That's when Pastor Lore's words came back to me: 'It's okay to cry. Your tears are a form of prayer.'

"And then God revealed to me what a difference those words from Pastor Lore made in the life of my family. I could have stopped going to church. My children could have been denied the opportunity to really know the Lord. God provided Pastor Lore to minister to me when I was hurting. He placed our daughters in the same class for that reason. I am very grateful."

> *Dear Heavenly Father, thank you for the gift of tears, as we pour out our hearts to you in prayer. And thank you for sending the right people to intervene in our lives, even before we know what our needs are. In the name of Jesus Christ we pray. Amen.*

SECTION THREE

UNEXPECTED GIFTS

16

Recover a Sense of Wonder about God

"Stop and consider God's wonders."

JOB 37:14

"Last spring my husband, Rick, and I were working in our three-acre yard transplanting some flowers from the front yard to the back," said Kathy. "We searched for a shady place and finally decided on an area behind our deck. Nothing had ever been planted in that spot before."

Rick said, "I started digging and about two inches down in the ground I found a tarnished piece of silver, smaller than my thumbnail. It was a teardrop-shaped charm or locket. As I rubbed it between my fingers to clean it off, I was incredulous to see our son's name engraved on it: Brian. I turned it over in my hand, and on the other side was engraved: Love.

"Kathy, look what I found!"

Rick said, "Kathy examined it closely and turned it over in her hand. When she looked up at me, she had a big smile. Her face sparkled from the tears rolling down her cheeks. Then she leaned over and gave me a great big kiss."

What made this discovery so special was that Rick and Kathy's son, Brian, had died in an auto accident seven years earlier.

"It looked like a charm that had fallen from someone's bracelet," explained Kathy. "It didn't belong to me, and Brian didn't have a girlfriend when he died. I have no idea where it came from, but it was a joyful moment for us, not sad at all. It was a gift of comfort from God and a wonderful reminder of Brian's love for us."

I knew the timing was right for Rick and Kathy's story when my husband read me a similar story from a book titled *Recapture the Wonder*[1] by Ravi Zacharias. The author states that our sense of wonder is a blessing from God, one that we should never lose sight of. He says that we all used to have a childlike sense of wonder, but for many of us, our awe of God becomes diminished through the years.

The author told a story about an elderly woman in Cambridge, England, whose picture appeared in the newspaper. She was kneeling beside a flowerbed with one hand raised high and a smile of glee across her face. As the woman dug up the soil to plant some flowers, she struck something. She dug her hands into the dirt, thinking it was a small stone, but saw something glistening. To her surprise, it was her wedding ring. She had lost it shortly after her husband died fifteen years earlier. A flood of memories bathed her soul. The ring brought back the feeling of decades of happiness spent with the one to whom she had committed her life. She was filled with a joy that she could not contain.

"That awe-filled experience is more than just an illustration to me," said the author. "It summarizes for me what life is intended to be—the thrill of wonder and the irresistible urge to share it. If one ring, a symbol, can stir the heart to such bounds of delight, how much more when we turn to the Shepherd of our souls and recover the wonder lost?"

> *Dear Heavenly Father, thank you for the unexpected gifts of comfort you give us. Help us to never lose that sense of awe and wonder in your miracle-working power. In the name of Jesus Christ we pray.*
> *Amen.*

---

1. Zacharias, Ravi. *Recapture the Wonder*. (Nashville: Thomas Nelson, Inc., 2003), 80-81.

17

Detours Can Turn into Blessings

God did not lead them on the road through the Philistine country, though that was shorter. . . . God led the people around by the desert road toward the Red Sea.

EXODUS 3:17-18

Oh, great! thought Joyce. *A great beginning to my day—a detour!*
Joyce drives from her home to work each day by the same route using several country back roads. She said, "One September day, I was feeling down. I sometimes get depressed during the fall season of the year because my only child died at that time of the year.

"The depression seemed to be worse this year," she continued. "To match my mood, the usual fall colors had been late in coming, and the colors have not been as brilliant as usual.

"I was making my way through the countryside when I came to a railroad crossing that was closed for repairs—a detour. I wasn't happy about it, but I found an alternate route. I've lived in this area all my life, but I couldn't remember when I had last been down the road I decided to take. As I came over a small rise, a spectacular scene unfolded before me: the most beautiful set of trees I have ever seen with vibrant fall colors. It took my breath away.

"And then it hit me. God sent me on that detour to bless me, to show me one of the beauties of his creation. It lifted my spirit and that feeling stayed with me throughout the day."

I was bowled over by Joyce's recognition that this small inconvenience was from God, and his sole purpose was to bless her and comfort her as she grieved for her daughter.

Can God create detours? Absolutely! This question was answered unequivocally for me in a Bible study class on the book of Exodus, the story of the Israelites as they were led from slavery out of Egypt. Listen to these words from Exodus 13:17-18, "God did not lead them on the road through the Philistine country, though that was shorter. . . . God led the people around by the desert road toward the Red Sea."

The Red Sea, of course, was the site of one of God's greatest displays of power: the parting of the waters so that the fleeing Israelites could pass on dry ground. Without a doubt, God planned that detour.

The next time you experience a detour, immediately pray to discern God's leading. Watch and wait to see if the Lord is working in an unexpected way. You may be in store for a blessing you never anticipated.

Dear Heavenly Father, we are impatient human beings! We want our minute-by-minute plans uninterrupted. Help us to stop and pray when our lives take a detour. Open our eyes and show us where you are working. In the name of Jesus Christ we pray. Amen.

18

The Perfect Gift

Thanks be to God for his indescribable gift!
2 CORINTHIANS 9:15

"I don't know anyone from Jasper, Indiana. What in the world could this be?"

It was 7:30 on the evening of December 16. My eighty-seven-year-old mother-in-law, Geletza, was in the family room of her home when she saw a UPS truck pull up to her house. She watched out the front window as the man carried a large white box to her front door.

When she got the box opened and saw what was inside, she was overcome with a flood of emotions—both happy and sad. It was a yellow quilt her mother had made more than sixty years before, a wedding gift to her brother, Gene, and his wife, Esther, in 1942. That quilt brought back bittersweet memories of Gene. He died in France in 1944 during World War II. He was only twenty-seven years old.

Esther remarried and had a family after Gene died, but Esther and Geletza stayed in close contact throughout the years. The last time Geletza talked to her was in March, nine months earlier. Esther was eighty-seven years old and very ill. "I want you to have that yellow quilt," said Esther, "the one your mother gave us for a wedding gift."

Geletza was the last person to talk to Esther. She died later that night.

Esther's granddaughter mailed the quilt with a letter that said, "I apologize that I'm just getting in touch with you. Enclosed is the quilt Grandma wanted you to have. She thought a lot of you and told me about Gene often. I think she always struggled with his death. I found the enclosed picture of Gene and knew she would want you to have it."

It was a picture of Gene standing proudly in his Army uniform next to his 1940 Ford.

Geletza didn't sleep well that night because of all the memories that quilt brought. It was a powerful connection to her family, something she could actually touch and hold in her hands.

Geletza showed me the quilt the next day. It looked like new, with its vibrant patches of color on a yellow background. Esther had stored it away after Gene's death, so it hadn't been used in six decades. She held it on her lap and touched it lovingly as she told me the story.

"I recognize some of the pieces in the quilt," she said. "I can remember Mom wearing dresses and aprons made from the different patterns of material. Mom was always working on a quilt. I can picture her sitting at the quilting frame, which was in a separate room in our house, large enough for four women to work at a time. The women took turns going to different homes to quilt in the wintertime. They started early in the morning and worked all day. I can't tell you how many hours it must have taken to make one quilt."

Geletza kept that quilt on her bed until she died a year later. Now it is a cherished family heirloom that will be passed down through the family.

Dear Heavenly Father, Geletza was going about her life doing ordinary things when you surprised her with something extraordinary. Esther's granddaughter needn't have apologized for taking nine months to send that quilt. It was the perfect unexpected Christmas gift, and it arrived in your perfect timing. You love to surprise your children with wonderful gifts that bring memories of our loved ones who are in heaven with you. It is in the name of Jesus we pray. Amen.

19

Wind beneath My Wings

"I carried you on eagles' wings and brought you to myself."
EXODUS 19:4

A young man named Scott gave his mother, Sandy, a very special birthday gift: a copy of the Bette Midler song, "Wind beneath My Wings." Scott attached a note that said, "Mom, this is your song. This is how I feel about you. You are the wind beneath my wings."

Sandy said, "That song was special to me after that."

Three months later the unthinkable happened: Scott died suddenly. He was only twenty-three years old. For Scott's funeral, a group of his friends put together a collection of his favorite songs, which included "Wind beneath My Wings."

Every year around the anniversary of their son's death, Sandy and her husband, Sam, go away for the weekend. Sandy said, "Sometimes it makes it easier to take our minds off things."

On one of those trips, they were driving and reminiscing about Scott. "Can you believe it's been seven years already?" asked Sam.

"No, it doesn't seem possible," she answered.

In the middle of their conversation, they realized that the song playing on the car radio was "Wind beneath My Wings."

Sandy said, "The tears started rolling down our cheeks. We knew that God's presence with us at that moment was real and very strong, and we thanked God for that gift.

"At first it was extremely difficult to hear that song, but as time goes on, it brings back good memories of Scott. Now, every time I hear that song, I consider it a wonderful gift from God, a reminder of Scott's love for me and God's love for me. God can take painful memories and with time turn them into wonderful gifts that we can cherish."

> *Dear Heavenly Father, it's painful to lose a loved one, and the loss of a child is perhaps the most painful of all. But we know that you suffered the same pain with the death of your only son on the cross. Remind us that you are acquainted with grief. When we suffer, you suffer with us. In the name of your son Jesus Christ, we pray. Amen.*

20

Foretaste of Heaven

But our citizenship is in heaven. And we eagerly await a Savior from there, the Lord Jesus Christ, who . . . will transform our lowly bodies so that they will be like his glorious body.

PHILIPPIANS 2:20-21

"When I tell people this, they don't believe me, but I know what I saw," said June, a friend of mine whose husband, Jim, had just died. "He had the most peaceful and happy look on his face I have ever seen," she assured me. "He looked thirty years younger, and all the lines in his face were gone."

Jim died unexpectedly in his sleep. He had not been well for several years, but it was still a terrible shock when June discovered he wasn't breathing that morning. Through the tears, she told me her amazing story about Jim's appearance after he died.

Is it possible that God gave June a foretaste of what her husband looked like in heaven? I didn't question her experience at all. In fact, God reminded me of similar stories people have shared with me.

John told me about his sister, Ruthie, who was stricken with polio as a baby. Ruthie struggled physically her whole life. When Ruthie died, John couldn't believe his eyes. "She didn't look like the seventy-year-old Ruthie I knew," he said. "She looked like a beautiful young lady, as she might have looked thirty years ago. As I stood there looking at her sweet face, the Lord said to me: 'If you think she looks good now, wait till you see her in heaven!'"

This physical transformation at the time of death was confirmed in one of the most powerful Christian books I have ever read: *The Hiding Place* by Corrie ten Boom. She and most of her family ended up in a concentration camp during World War II. Corrie and her sister, Betsie, experienced all the horrors of that life, but they also witnessed God's presence in miraculous ways.

The morning came when Betsie was so sick that she could not make it outside for roll call. Two orderlies from the camp hospital took her away on a stretcher. (The "hospital" was a place for dying, not healing.) The next morning Corrie ran to the hospital and peered through a window at Betsie. Corrie described the emaciated figure on the bed as "a carving in old yellow ivory. There was no clothing on the figure. I could see each ivory rib, and the outline of the teeth through the parchment cheeks."[1]

Two nurses lifted the corners of the sheet and carried her lifeless body out of the room. Corrie ran around to the back of the building where she found Betsie's body among dozens lining the wall. She wrote:

> I raised my eyes to Betsie's face. "Lord Jesus—what have you done? Oh, Lord, what are you saying? What are you giving me?" For there lay Betsie, her eyes closed as if in sleep, her face full and young. The care lines, the grief lines, the deep hollows of hunger and disease were simply gone. . . . This was the Betsie of heaven, bursting with joy and health. Even her hair was graciously in place as if an angel had ministered to her. . . . Now what tied me to Betsie was the hope of heaven.[2]

Scripture promises us as believers of Jesus Christ that our citizenship is ultimately in heaven. There, Jesus "will transform our lowly bodies so that they will be like his glorious body" (Philippians 2:21). We claim that promise.

Dear Heavenly Father, thank you for these miracles of transformation, where we are given a glimpse of what our loved ones might look like in heaven. In the name of Jesus Christ we pray. Amen.

---

1. Ten Boom, Corrie. *The Hiding Place* (Grand Rapids. Chosen Books, 1971), 197.

2. Ibid. 198-199.

21

A Father's Day Gift

*You received the Spirit of adoption by whom
we cry out Abba Father.*

ROMANS 8:15

"This will be the first Father's Day without my dad," said Michelle. "He was diagnosed with Stage 4 liver cancer last July. His prognosis was poor—six months to one year. He had never been ill, so it was a shock to the family that his life was going to be cut short. He didn't live as long as predicted. He passed away in November, only four months after the diagnosis.

"This Father's Day will be difficult because I miss him very much. He was a religious man with a strong faith, so I know he is with the Lord."

"Dad lived in Canton, Ohio, so we corresponded a lot by e-mail. Before the cancer, he never expressed his feelings to me face to face, except through e-mails, so those messages were precious. After the diagnosis, he began telling me in person how he felt.

"In May, six months after he died, I was sitting at my computer when I discovered I had saved a file containing e-mail messages from my dad. I went back and read some of them, which made me miss him even more. While reading those messages, I thought, *I'll just send him a message to his old e-mail address and see what happens."*

Dad, I miss you more than you will ever know. What I would give to hear your voice again. I love you. Michelle.

She clicked the "send" button and within minutes, she received a message back: "undeliverable."

"I sobbed, all the while knowing it was expected. At that moment, I heard 'Michelle' softly called out behind me. I turned quickly to respond, to find no one in the room with me. Without a doubt, I got my wish. I heard Dad's voice again. God does work in mysterious ways."

That message wasn't undeliverable after all. God received it.

I heard a similar story from a woman named Shirley, who was very close to her father. "He passed away five years ago," she said. "I miss him very much, but I thank God he is in heaven and no longer in pain. On my dad's birthday, I was especially sad. As I drove to work that morning, I stopped at a traffic light when all of a sudden, I heard a voice say, 'I'll be your father.' Then a few seconds later I heard, 'I'll be your Abba Father.'"

Shirley said, "That voice was so clear that I turned around and looked into the back seat of the car. I thought someone was in the car with me. Then I knew without a doubt that God had spoken to me. I cried and rejoiced that he would speak to me like that when I was grieving so. Now I can feel his help and presence in a powerful way throughout the day."

Shirley found out that the word "Abba" is a more intimate term for "father," more like the word "daddy." She quoted Romans 8:15, "You received the Spirit of adoption by whom we cry out Abba Father."

Another Bible verse that came to mind for this story was: "Nothing is impossible with God" (Luke 1:37). Our God is a God of compassion, who consoles us in our grief, and, indeed, nothing is impossible for him.

Dear Heavenly Father, Thank you for all the unexpected gifts you give us when we are grieving. You know exactly what we need. In the name of Jesus Christ we pray. Amen.

SECTION FOUR

SIGNS OF COMFORT

22

A Mother's Prayer for a Sign

*Ask the Lord your God for a sign,
whether in the deepest depths or in the highest heights.*

ISAIAH 7:10

It was early May when Dutch and Kathy found this note from their twenty-eight-year-old son, David, tucked in their suitcase:

"Dear Mom and Dad, I want you to know how much I love you. I thank my Father in heaven for letting you be my parents. Love, Davy"

His signature was followed by three crosses and the early Christian fish symbol. He always added those symbols after his name as a way of witnessing to people about his strong faith in Jesus Christ.

Dutch and Kathy had just arrived at a condo in Gatlinburg, Tennessee, for a vacation.

"Let's call Davy to come join us for the rest of our vacation," said Kathy. They loved the Smoky Mountains and visited there nearly every year for thirty years. "Our family had many happy memories there."

David arrived at noon the next day, and they spent the rest of the day together. "It was one of the happiest times we can remember with Davy. He was our one and only child. We lost six babies to miscarriages, but then the Lord poured everything good into this one child."

It was 11:30 PM as they prepared to go to bed. "Thank you for asking me to spend this special time with you," said David as he hugged and kissed his parents goodnight. "I love you."

The next morning at 9 AM, Kathy went to David's bedside to awaken him. As soon as she touched him, she knew the awful truth: David had died in his sleep.

The next few hours were a blur of activity: Kathy called 911; the paramedics arrived; David was pronounced dead. Since he died unexpectedly at such a young age, the police investigated. The coroner said he appeared to have died many hours earlier, probably soon after he had gone to bed the night before. David's body was taken to the hospital where authorities later determined he died of natural causes.

A lot of paperwork had to be completed before Dutch and Kathy could leave for the long, lonely trip home. "We were absolutely numb from the shock and grief," said Kathy. "I felt like my heart had been ripped out. I remember thinking how Jesus' mother must have hurt at the loss of her only son. As Dutch drove, I held Davy's driver's license, looking at his picture on it as I prayed. I was so weak and tired. I prayed, 'Lord, I know my child is with you, but I need a sign, any little sign, to get me through this first night without my son.'"

As they drove down the interstate, Dutch pulled into the left lane to pass a semitrailer, a tandem, with two trailers hooked together. Kathy glanced to the right as they passed, and there was the answer to her prayer: In the dirt on the back of that first trailer, someone had drawn with their finger three crosses and a fish.

God knew David's trademark signature. No other sign could have had the same impact.

"That sign got me through that first night without my son," said Kathy. "We've had numerous signs and visions since then confirming Davy's presence with the Lord."

> *Dear God, thank you for answering Kathy's prayer for a sign in such a beautiful, comforting way, blessed assurance that he is, indeed, with you. We take comfort in knowing that your heart breaks with every tear we shed. In the name of Jesus Christ we pray. Amen.*

23

The Miracle of the Rosebuds

He performs signs and wonders in the heavens and on the earth.

DANIEL 6:27

Lyle was Darlene's firstborn son. When he was eight years old, Darlene and her husband, Bob, adopted a son named Warren. Four years later Darlene was delighted to discover she was pregnant with another child. After a difficult birth, Ryan was born severely handicapped with cerebral palsy.

"When Ryan was two and a half years old," said Darlene, "my thirty-nine-year old husband developed cancer and died within three months. I was left with three sons, ages fifteen, seven, and two and a half. Our church enveloped us with love during that traumatic time, and it was there that I met my future husband, Bill, who became a wonderful blessing in my life.

"During the next ten years we were a very busy family with the kids' activities. Lyle grew up to be a talented and gifted musician and artist, while Ryan struggled physically and was hospitalized many times throughout the years. He never had use of any of his limbs, nor could he talk, yet, he had a wonderful smile and seemed to be quite intelligent. He found ways to let us know his needs, and he understood what we spoke to him. In spite of all his handicaps, he was never a burden to us. Ryan was fourteen years old when he died unexpectedly in his sleep. We all had a difficult time coping with the loss.

"Six years later our family planned a long-awaited reunion in Minnesota on some lake-front property. We believe that's where our oldest son, Lyle, contracted a water parasite. During the next few months, millions of deadly parasites attacked his body. It was a death sentence.

"During his last days I gave him nightly back rubs. One night I told him I was praying for a sign that would tell me when he found his little brother, Ryan, in heaven.

"A few nights later I had a dream about a miniature rose bush I had purchased. It was sickly and about to die, but then it was healthy again and produced two red rosebuds. When I told Lyle about my dream, we wondered if this could be a sign."

Lyle died two weeks later in his mother's arms. He was only thirty-three years old.

At the funeral home, a long-time friend and her two daughters approached Darlene. "They had babysat my children when they were young. I was so glad to see them. When I greeted the older daughter, she said, 'I don't know why, but I was compelled to stop and buy you these.'

"She was carrying something in green florist paper," said Darlene. "I pulled back the paper to reveal two red rosebuds. My happy heart sang: 'I know why.'"

In the midst of Darlene's heartache, God gave her this beautiful sign of comfort that her two sons were in heaven together.

Thank you, Lord, for this miracle of comfort in the midst of loss, confirmation that you still "perform signs and wonders in the heavens and on the earth" (Daniel 6:27). In the name of Jesus Christ we pray. Amen.

24

Give God the Credit for Miraculous Signs

I thought it good to declare the signs and wonders that the Most High God has worked for me.

DANIEL 4:2

"Ron had a passion for hummingbirds," said his friend, Sabrina. "It was quite an experience for me and my husband, Rick, to watch them from his screened-in patio and hear the sounds they made. About twenty hummingbirds came to feed every evening. Ron taught us about hummingbirds and their habits, and you could hear the excitement and passion in his voice.

"Unfortunately, a few short years into our friendship, Ron passed away. Rick and I were given the opportunity to purchase Ron's truck. We drove it home, an odd experience because Ron's scent was still in it. We both talked about Ron and reminisced about our lives together. We parked the truck in the garage for the night and that was that, so we thought.

"The next time we had to leave, we took the car and never mentioned driving the truck. It became a common occurrence to drive the car instead of the truck. Finally, we admitted to each other that we were uncomfortable in it. We missed our friend very much. Even after talking about it, we couldn't bring ourselves to drive it. We began to think that purchasing the truck had been a mistake.

"One day as I sat at my computer looking out our big picture window, a hummingbird flew up, hovered at the window for a moment, and then darted out of sight. Rick and I were excited. We had lived in that house for thirteen years and never before had a hummingbird visitor. We bought a feeder, hung it outside our window, and hoped it would come back to feed, but we didn't have high hopes that we would ever see it again. But the next day the bird was back feeding. This took place every evening for a few more days. Then he flew off one evening never to be seen again.

"Before this experience, I was very skeptical of stories about signs. When people hurt deeply and miss their loved ones and friends so terribly, it's easy to be taken in by an event like this. But since this experience, I am now a firm believer in signs. God knew that we would recognize that sign immediately. I choose to believe that God sent the hummingbird to comfort us. We began driving the truck, and now we enjoy the thoughts it brings of our friendship with Ron."

I put Sabrina's hummingbird story aside. The next morning when I checked my e-mail messages, there was one from an online friend named Dave. I couldn't believe it when I opened his message and found the most exquisite pictures of . . . you guessed it . . . hummingbirds! His short note said, "I took these close-up pictures of hummingbirds at my backyard feeder and wanted to share them with you."

I have never had anyone send me pictures of hummingbirds. For those pictures to arrive the morning after Sabrina's message was not a coincidence. It was a sign from the Lord that he wanted me to write this story.

Dear Heavenly Father, stories of miraculous signs are common in the Bible, but today we look at signs and say, "What a nice coincidence!" Open our eyes to the signs and wonders all around us and let us give you the credit. In the name of Jesus Christ we pray. Amen.

25

The Miracle of the White Dove

"The Holy Spirit . . . will teach you all things."
JOHN 14:26

My father-in-law died the night before Thanksgiving. He had been ill, but it was still unexpected, and some of us were troubled by the fact that he died alone in the hospital two hours after the family had visited him. I didn't understand why that happened, and I prayed for God to give me some peace about that.

The funeral was the following Saturday. The next day our family sat in our dining room during our first Sunday dinner without Dad. We talked about the funeral and shared happy memories. I was sitting directly across from a picture window in the dining room. About halfway through dinner I said, "Look! There's a white bird out there—completely white!" I jumped from my chair to get a closer look at it. "I've never seen a bird like that in my life. Is it a white dove?"

Our whole family gathered at the picture window. My husband grabbed the camera and took pictures of it. We watched the bird for the next half hour as it flitted from one branch to another and ate from the birdfeeder.

My husband is a bird lover. In the twenty-eight years we've lived in our home, we've never seen a bird like that. I called a friend, who is an expert on birds, a hobby she has pursued for nearly forty years.

In fact, she leads bird-watching tours at state parks. I told her we took pictures, and she wanted to see them. When we had the pictures developed, I took them to her. "No," she said. "I've never seen a bird like that around here."

I thought, *Could this be some kind of a sign?* I prayed that the Holy Spirit would reveal to me the meaning of this, claiming Jesus' promise in John 14:26, "The Holy Spirit will teach you all things." I watched and waited for an answer.

The next afternoon I sat in my family room next to a pile of books and started going through them. One immediately jumped out at me. On the cover was a breathtaking picture of a white dove in flight. Someone had loaned me the book weeks earlier. I had never gotten around to reading it, but the Holy Spirit led me to pick it up at exactly the right time in response to my prayer for understanding. The book is called *The Holy Spirit: The Boundless Energy of God* by Ron Roth.[1]

As I skimmed through the book, I was reminded that the image of the dove has long been a symbol for the Holy Spirit, based on Luke 3:21-22 when Jesus was baptized. It says, "Heaven was opened and the Holy Spirit descended on him in bodily form like a dove."

Could it be that the white dove in our yard was a sign from God that my father-in-law was with us in spirit as we shared family memories at our first meal without him?

In another section of the book, I was reminded that the white dove is the traditional symbol of peace.[2] I think it was God's way of assuring us that we should be at peace about his dying without us being there and to know that he hadn't been alone. Jesus was with him when he passed from this life onto the next. Believers have the promise of eternal life and a glorious reunion in heaven.

Dear Heavenly Father, thank you for the answer to my prayer for understanding. You gave us a gift of comfort and peace, the kind of peace that surpasses all human understanding. In the name of Jesus Christ we pray. Amen.

---

1. Roth, Ron. *Holy Spirit: The Boundless Energy of God* (Carlsbad: Hay House, Inc. 2000).

2. Ibid, p. 32.

26

He Comforts Us in Our Troubles

Praise be to the God and Father of our Lord Jesus Christ, the Father of compassion and the God of all comfort, who comforts us in all our troubles.

2 CORINTHIANS 1:3-4

It appears that God likes white dove stories because several people contacted me after I wrote about the white dove that appeared at our house after my father-in-law died. I received an e mail message from a woman named Debby, who remembered a story from her childhood. She wrote: "My grandmother had a very dear friend, whom we always called Miss B. She was married at an early age. She and her husband were from Greece, and it was an arranged marriage. He was much older, but they were devoted to each other and eventually had six sons.

"Mr. B passed away, leaving her with the six boys, some grown and on their own, a few still at home, and a Greek import shop to run. She was devastated and concerned about the future. The oldest son assured her that he would handle the business and take care of her.

"But the most reassuring thing was the white dove that appeared at her backyard feeder the day after Mr. B passed away. She had never seen it in the yard before, even though they were birdwatchers and had bird feeders for many years. She believes to this day that God sent that dove to remind her of his presence and to help her through that difficult time. She found the strength she needed to make decisions and come to peace with his passing. The dove came every day for about a month and then never returned. She was saddened by its departure, but she felt confident she could carry on, and she has.

"When my grandmother passed away, Miss B became a second grandmother to me. Miss B is now in her eighties. She lives far away from me, and she is not in the best of health, but we always visit her when we go home. She still lives in the same house, and sometimes our conversations turn to the white dove that comforted her in the difficult days. I only hope that when her time comes that God will send the white dove to comfort my family."

Dear Heavenly Father, Thank you for the many different ways you speak to us. Open our eyes and help us recognize the wonderful gifts of comfort you provide, signs of your faithfulness to us. In the name of Jesus we pray. Amen.

SECTION FIVE

MIRACLES OF NATURE

27

A Sign of God's Faithfulness

"I have set my rainbow in the clouds, and it will be a sign of the covenant between me and the earth."

GENESIS 9:14

My husband and I visited our daughter Shelley in Seattle, Washington, where we took in some of the sights, including an elevator ride up to the top of the Space Needle. It was built for the 1962 World's Fair and is the most-visited attraction in Seattle. The observation tower offers a panoramic view of the city, including Puget Sound and the snow-covered Cascade Mountains in the distance.

We decided to have lunch in the revolving restaurant atop the Space Needle. In a little more than an hour, we made a complete revolution, seeing the city from all directions. As we sat there enjoying the view, our conversation turned to my mother-in-law, who had passed away six months earlier. She had died rather suddenly, and my daughter Shelley was still troubled by the fact that she died just two hours before her plane arrived in Indianapolis. Shelley was on her way home for Christmas and had not seen her grandmother for seven months.

"I don't understand why Grandma died before I had a chance to see her. I'm kind of mad at God about that," she said.

"Yes, that's hard to understand," I agreed.

At that exact moment in our conversation, I turned to look out the window, and the view took my breath away. "Look at that!" I said. "It's a rainbow!"

Take my word for it. You haven't experienced a rainbow until you have seen one from the top of the Space Needle. We could see the complete arc, stretching over the landscape. We got our cameras out and starting snapping pictures. People from the opposite side of the restaurant came over to our side to take pictures. We watched for the next fifteen or twenty minutes as the rainbow slowly faded from view.

As we got past the excitement of seeing it, I said, "Shelley, I think this was a sign from God to give you some peace about not seeing Grandma before she died."

To Christians, the rainbow is a sign of God's faithfulness to us. It comes from Genesis 9, the story of Noah after he and his family came out of the ark after the great flood. God promised never again to destroy the world by flood. To seal this promise, He said, "I have set my rainbow in the clouds, and it will be a sign of the covenant between me and the earth. (Gen. 9:13)

The rainbow is a sign that God is faithful and trustworthy throughout all generations.

> *Dear Heavenly Father, you could not have chosen a more beautiful symbol of your faithfulness to us than the rainbow. Thank you for this miracle of nature, in your perfect timing to comfort Shelley in her grief. In the name of Jesus Christ we pray. Amen.*

28

A Sweet Sign of Remembrance

"Therefore the Lord himself will give you a sign."

ISAIAH 7:14

"My husband's grandfather passed away in February," said Michelle. "A few weeks later during the Easter season, we purchased an Easter lily in his memory to be displayed at their church.

"After the service on Easter, we took our lily home. Someone told us if we planted it outdoors, it would come up each year. Later that day, we planted it on the south side of our home near the back door that we go in and out of all the time. Apparently we don't have a green thumb, because as the summer progressed, the lily gradually died."

As that first Christmas without Grandpa approached, Michelle said he was continually in their thoughts.

"On December 22 I walked out the back door and was shocked to see the Easter lily had emerged from the ground. In fact, it was six or eight inches tall! I hadn't seen it the day before. It was there for several days, through Christmas. Then the lily died and never returned."

We here in Indiana know that flowers don't usually appear in December. Even more extraordinary is that December 22 was especially significant for another reason: It was Grandpa's birthday!

Michelle said, "Only God could have arranged that perfect timing. It was a one-time miracle. Something that appeared to be dead came back to life. God chose that very special sign to comfort us."

It was no accident that God chose to use the Easter lily for this miracle, a symbol of new life, the resurrection of Jesus Christ, and the promise of eternal life.

> *Dear Heavenly Father, thank you for this gift of comfort to Michelle and her family. Only you can arrange for a flower to bloom in December in Indiana. You are an awesome God! In the name of Jesus Christ we pray. Amen.*

29

God Answers Out of the Whirlwind

Then the Lord answered Job out of the whirlwind.

JOB 38:1

Joyce, whose 21-year-old daughter, Autumn, died several years ago, still has periods of intense grief. Autumn was her only child.

"I was upset because of some problems in my life," said Joyce. "I miss Autumn ten times more when things go wrong. I got on my riding lawn mower, crying as I drove back and forth across the yard, 'Oh, Autumn, where are you? Are you with God?'

"Immediately, a gust of wind came and the butterfly windsock that I thought was lost during the winter flew out of the gutter and rose with the wind. That is the fastest response from God I've ever had! Praise God!"

For added measure, the symbol God used, the butterfly, could not have been more appropriate. The butterfly has become a symbol of new life to Christians. It is seen more and more in our Easter celebrations, and sometimes butterflies are released at funerals, a symbol of eternal life when we are transformed into beautiful new beings in heaven.

"The windsock floated high in the air as I rode back and forth across the yard, probably for a period of ten minutes or so. I drove around the corner of the house to another part of the yard where I couldn't see it. Later when I returned, the wind sock was nowhere to be seen."

The next morning during my prayer time, I prayed for confirmation to write Joyce's story. I picked up my Bible and a study book called *The Grand Sweep*, by J. Ellsworth Kalas,[1] with assigned Bible readings and commentary for each day. That day's lesson began with a reading from Job 38, where God comes to answer Job's complaints. The very first verse said: "Then the Lord answered Job out of the whirlwind." (Job 38:1)

That's exactly what happened to Joyce. God answered her out of the whirlwind! I never could have found that verse in the Bible on my own, but God, in his miraculous way, showed it to me at the precise moment I needed to see it. I agree with Joyce: Praise God!

Dear Heavenly Father, thank you that you come to us in miraculous ways when we need you most. This story is a beautiful confirmation of your promise of eternal life and that Autumn is, indeed, in heaven with you. In the name of Jesus Christ we pray. Amen.

---

1. Kalas, J. Ellsworth. *The Grand Sweep* (Nashville: Abingdon Press, 1996), 128.

30

God Comforts on Special Days

When you see this, your heart will rejoice.
ISAIAH 66:14

"My father passed away in April," began Nancy. "My employer sent a hibiscus plant to the funeral home for the viewing. When we received it, there was only one dark orange-red bloom on it. The next day when we returned for the funeral, the bloom was gone.

"I took the plant home with me, hoping to keep it alive since I'm known to have a 'black thumb.' I called friends to find out how to care for it and received all kinds of suggestions. I watered it regularly and fertilized it every two weeks. No blossoms. I set it out on the patio for the summer. Still nothing. I was disappointed when it continued to be without the beautiful flowers I knew it could produce.

"On a Sunday afternoon in June I decided to do a little shopping. For some reason, I went out on the back deck to walk around to the car in the front of the house, something I normally don't do. I looked down at that plant as I walked by and there was a beautiful orange-yellow bloom, only one, a little bit lighter in color than the original bloom. It was a gift from God, because it appeared on a special day—Father's Day—the first Father's Day without my dad. The next day the bloom wilted and fell to the floor."

That wasn't the end of the gift of comfort to Nancy. "We moved to a different house in September," said Nancy. "I placed the plant on the screened porch. That flower bloomed again on another special day—September 11, Daddy's birthday! Once more, it was a single bloom, which was gone the next day.

"When the weather got colder in October, I moved it inside to my living room and put it by the porch window. No more blooms appeared until a November morning—Thanksgiving! Again, there was a single faded yellow bloom. The next morning it had dropped to the floor. The same scenario played out on Christmas."

During that first year after her dad's death, that flower bloomed only on those special days when she missed him the most.

> *Dear Lord, thank you for showing us that you care about the details of our lives, even to the point of arranging when flowers bloom. You comfort us in such tender ways when we are grieving. You bring to life your words in Matthew 5:4: "Blessed are those who mourn, for they will be comforted." In the name of Jesus Christ we pray. Amen.*

31

A Rainbow Straight From Heaven

A rainbow . . . encircled the throne.

REVELATION 4:3

My friend, Rosie, had a special affinity for rainbows. She told me several stories throughout our thirty-five-year friendship of rainbows appearing at special times in her life, usually as a source of comfort. It is no surprise, then, that a rainbow appeared after her funeral.

Rosie's family and friends said their final goodbyes at the cemetery and headed back to their small country church for the funeral dinner. As they headed west, one of the grandkids looked out the car window excitedly and said, "Look at that rainbow! Have you ever seen a rainbow like that?"

Witnesses said it wasn't a "normal" rainbow with an arc across the sky like we usually see; instead, it encircled the sun, like a halo, and then there was a second circular rainbow out farther from the first. It was fainter, almost like a shadow of the first rainbow.

As they watched the spectacle on their drive back to the church, Rosie's husband, Jerry, said, "I asked for a sign that she was in heaven. That's it."

How many of you have ever witnessed a circular rainbow? I didn't even know such a thing was possible until I found a reference to it in my Bible.

Most people are familiar with the Genesis 9 story of God showing Noah a rainbow after the flood, a sign of God's faithfulness to us, but do you know the story of the rainbow in the Book of Revelation? As I read this passage, it gave me goose bumps because it involves a description of heaven and a circular rainbow. In my Bible this section is entitled "The Throne in Heaven."

> "To him who overcomes, I will give the right to sit with me on my throne . . ." I looked, and there before me was a door standing open in heaven . . . At once I was in the Spirit, and there before me was a throne in heaven with someone sitting on it . . . A rainbow . . . encircled the throne (Revelation 3:21, 4:1-3)[1]

Dear Heavenly Father, thank you for sending this perfect sign of comfort to Rosie's family, a reminder of your faithfulness to us. In the name of Jesus Christ we pray. Amen.

---

1. *Life Application Study Bible*, NIV (Grand Rapids: Zondervan Publishing House, 1991), 2307.

32

Memorial Day Remembrance

"Do this in remembrance of me."
LUKE 22:19

What does Memorial Day mean to you? For some people it's just another national holiday. The mail isn't delivered, the courthouse is closed, you can't go to the bank to get your check cashed, and you can't renew your driver's license. We grumble about these loss of services rather than remember those who have gone before us.

Memorial Day began as a custom to honor the Civil War dead. It was expanded to commemorate the deaths of anyone who served in the military. Throughout the years, it became a time for decorating the graves of any of our loved ones, a time to remember all those who have passed on before us. Some "old timers" still call it Decoration Day.

A 73-year-old friend of mine named Eva has kept that tradition alive in her family. She and her sister-in-law, Mabel, spend the day decorating graves every year. She said, "It's a tough day, very emotional, but I try to think about the good memories. I have a peace that somehow they know I am there remembering them.

"Memorial Day last year was a dark, rainy day as we began our trip," said Eva. "All the graves we visit are in central Indiana. Mabel and I went first to Oak Hill Cemetery near Kirklin to the grave of one of my brothers. It was pouring rain on the way there, with the windshield wipers going full speed. But the moment we pulled into that cemetery, the rain stopped just long enough for us to decorate his grave.

"Next, we traveled to a cemetery in Sheridan to the graves of another brother and Mabel's uncle. It poured rain all the way there, too, but when we got out of the car, the rain again stopped.

"We went on to another little cemetery outside of Sheridan to the graves of Mabel's mom and dad. It was the same scenario: Rain all the way there, clearing off just long enough for us to leave the flowers and get back in the car.

"We stopped at Carey Cemetery between Noblesville and Elwood. My husband and two sons are buried there. My husband was a veteran, so I always put a flag on his grave too. Again, it rained all the way there, but it cleared off just long enough to decorate their graves.

"Finally, we headed to a little cemetery in Tetersburg where my mom and dad are buried. Again, it was the same scenario: The rain stopped just long enough for us to decorate the graves."

Eva giggled and said, "Wasn't that a nice thing for God to do for us? I guess you could call it a miracle!"

"Yes, Eva, I think that was a miracle," I answered.

Dear Heavenly Father, you call us to honor the saints who have gone before us. Thank you for Memorial Day, this special holiday to remember our veterans and other loved ones. In the name of Jesus Christ we pray. Amen.

33

Butterflies: A Symbol of New Life

If anyone is in Christ, he is a new creation; old things have passed away; behold, all things have become new.

2 CORINTHIANS 5:17

On Memorial Day in 1992 Fran and her 16-year-old daughter Heather went to the Plainview Cemetery in Colfax, Indiana, to decorate the graves of two special people. Fran said, "My mother-in-law passed away in January, 1991, and then one year later in January, 1992, her daughter Sherry died a violent death. She was only 43 years old. They are buried side by side. We spent some time planting flowers and reminiscing about my mother-in-law and Sherry. I removed the faded artificial flowers left from the winter, but I couldn't bear to throw them away, so I put them in the bucket I had brought with me and took them home."

Fran had bought enough flowers to plant some at her house in her enclosed back yard. Heather was sitting on the back step as her mother planted the flowers. "The memories were very strong," said Fran. "It was especially difficult for Heather because she was very close to her Aunt Sherry."

Heather said, "I can't believe Aunt Sherry is gone. I thought she was invincible, that she would never die."

As they talked, a monarch butterfly flitted around the old artificial flowers from the cemetery. They thought that was odd because there were real flowers in the yard, but the butterfly was attracted to the artificial ones for some reason. "Mom," said Heather, "do you think the butterfly is a sign that Aunt Sherry is in heaven?"

Heather prayed for the butterfly to land on her hand if it was a sign from God, and it did! After a few moments, it flew away. Then Heather prayed the same prayer again, and once more, the butterfly landed on her hand.

Fran said, "God's presence was extremely powerful. Heather and I both thought it was reassurance that Sherry was with the Lord. We knew we would see her again in heaven."

I've had several people tell me miracle stories about butterflies, all related to the death of a loved one, as if God was comforting them in their grief.

Second Corinthians 5:17 offers a wonderful promise from God: "If anyone is in Christ, he is a new creation; old things have passed away; all things have become new." For Christians butterflies are a symbol for this new creation, because of their miraculous life cycle. They begin as caterpillars. When they are full grown, they form a chrysalis, a protective covering. On the surface, they appear to be dead, but this delicate process changes a caterpillar into a butterfly with wings and beautiful colors.

This metamorphosis can be compared to the change in a person who accepts Christ. He becomes a new creation. It can also be a symbol for eternal life when we are transformed into beautiful new beings in heaven.

Dear Heavenly Father, thank you for comforting us when we are grieving and for the incredible promise that we will become a new creation when we pass from this life to eternal life with you. In the name of Jesus Christ we pray. Amen.

34

Lilacs and Lilies

It will burst into bloom. . . . They will see the glory of the Lord, the splendor of our God.

ISAIAH 35:2

In my daily walks in the springtime, I enjoy the sight of flowers, bushes, and trees in full bloom. One of the bushes I especially enjoy is the lilac. I can smell the distinctive fragrance of lilacs even before the bush comes into view.

Each year when they bloom, God reminds me of a story about a very special lilac bush. It was a Mother's Day gift from twelve-year-old Doug to his mother, Vicki.

Vicki didn't have much of a green thumb, but she loved that bush. She babied it along, but for the next four springs, she was disappointed when it either didn't bloom at all or produced only one or two blooms.

She was excited the next spring close to Mother's Day when she walked through her back yard and saw that bush loaded with blooms. She counted the purple blossoms—sixteen of them. Only then did she realize what a gift God had given her.

Mother's Day that year was an especially difficult one

for Vicki because Doug, her only child, had died six months earlier. The grief was almost more than she could bear. The fact that the bush was in full bloom on Mother's Day was a miracle, but even more amazing was the fact that Doug would have been sixteen years old that year.

Vicki said, "Doug knew how much I loved that bush because it was a gift from him. He was saying, 'Mom, I'm okay.' No other sign could have had the same impact. God used this miracle to draw me closer to him, to remind me that he shared in my grief," she continued. "I knew I had to have God in my life to make it through that time. This was his way of assuring me he was there."

God reached down and touched that bush to give Vicki this wonderful Mother's Day gift—the assurance that Doug was living in eternal life with him. That bush has been loaded with blooms every year since then.

After this story appeared in the newspaper, one of Doug's aunts called me and continued the story. She said, "When Doug died, Vicki wanted us to take a plant home with us from the funeral home. I chose a peace lily.

"That lily didn't bloom for several years after Doug's death, and even then, it had only one bloom. But the day that one bloom appeared was a miracle because it was Doug's seventeenth birthday. We knew it was another sign from God that Doug was with him."

The fact that God chose to send this sign through a peace lily is even more amazing, because a sense of peace was exactly what the family needed on that special day. We cannot escape adversity in this life, but we can experience the peace that can only come from God.

> *Dear Heavenly Father, thank you for the tender ways you comfort us when we are grieving. Your heart aches with every tear we shed. Help us to be open to your consolation. In the name of Jesus Christ we pray. Amen.*

SECTION SIX

ANGELS ARE MINISTERING SPIRITS

35

Message for a Grieving Child

The angels said, "Why do you seek the living among the dead?"
LUKE 24:5

"Every Saturday my mother and I followed the same ritual," said Lu. "We went to the cemetery to pull weeds around my father's grave. My father died when I was two-and-a-half years old," she continued. "My only remembrance of him was not a very happy one—an image of my dead father lying in a casket.

"On one of those Saturday morning visits, when I was six years old, I was especially sad because the children at school had been teasing me because I didn't have a father. As I sat there wishing I had a daddy, two angels descended from above. They were very large, powerful beings, men clothed in long robes surrounded by a luminous bright light. One stood on each side of his grave. Then I saw a vision of my father as he came up out of the grave and stood between them. My father had a pleasant, peaceful expression on his face, just the way I remembered him. Those angels took him by the hand, one on each side, and they ascended into heaven.

"My mother couldn't see those angels. They were meant only for me."

Lu described to her mother what she had seen, but she was troubled about one thing. "Daddy didn't have any shoes on," she said.

Her mother reassured her. "The dead are many times buried without their shoes. Don't let that bother you." Lu's question about the shoes was proof to her mother that God had, indeed, given her daughter this vision.

Lu said, "Isn't it wonderful that God chose to speak to me about eternal life that way, showing such kindness to a grieving child? It was a personal message from God that my father was no longer dead in that casket. The teasing didn't hurt anymore because I knew my father was alive in heaven, and I had the assurance that I would be with him someday too."

The women who went to the tomb to anoint Jesus' body were also grieving. They, too, saw angels described as "two men in shining garments." The angels asked, "Why do you seek the living among the dead?" (Luke 24:4-5)

The angels Lu witnessed demonstrated the same message without actually speaking the words: "Why do you seek the living among the dead?"

Dear Heavenly Father, thank you that you used your heavenly messengers to speak to a child about grief and eternal life in a way she could understand. No matter what age we are, you comfort us. Thank you for Lu's willingness to share this experience with others for your glory, honor, and praise. In the name of Jesus Christ we pray. Amen.

36

Guardian Angel Brings Strength and Comfort

The angel of the Lord encamps around those who fear him.

PSALM 34:7

"Charlie and Sherry, I have some bad news. I have lung cancer and it has spread to the lymph nodes. My doctor says I may not live more than three months."

That phone call from Charlie's mother started an emotional roller coaster for the whole family. Sherry said, "I loved her very much. She was just like a mother to me. In fact, I called her Mom."

Sherry and Charlie made the ninety-minute trip to visit her the following Saturday. It was an emotional day and very late when they began the drive home. They didn't walk in the door until 2 AM.

"We were both exhausted mentally and physically," said Sherry. "Charlie got up before I did the next morning and went to the kitchen to make coffee. I was lying in bed praying and crying. Part of the burden was that I knew Mom was not a Christian. She was not affiliated with any church or religion. I prayed: 'Lord, she is such a good person. Let us have time together so she can get to know you.'

"I closed my eyes and put my hand over my face, still praying and crying. Then I had a terrifying vision of black, threatening clouds just churning, but out of the midst of those clouds an angel appeared, gently floating down toward me holding her hands out in front of her with the palms up. Around her was the most intense bright light, like no light I had ever seen.

"I remember noticing first her delicate hands and then her soft, pretty face. Her skin was like alabaster. She had wings of sheer gold, which surprised me because I had always seen angels pictured with feathers. She had long, flowing hair of a color I can't describe. It wasn't gold, red, or brown, but a combination of all those colors. She was wearing a long, sheer dress with vivid, vibrant colors—different shades of purple, rose and blue. She didn't speak, but simply knelt down by the side of the bed, put her hands together and prayed for several moments until she slowly faded away."

Sherry went to the kitchen and told Charlie, "I've just seen an angel."

He patted her on the shoulder and said, "It's okay, Honey. You're just tired and upset."

"The next weekend Mom came to our house for dinner," Sherry continued. "It was early spring, and we were sitting outside talking when she said something completely unexpected.

"Sherry, you won't believe this, but I saw you in a dream this week."

"Oh?" said Sherry.

"Yes. You brought an angel to me. She was extremely pretty, with beautiful, long hair and a long dress of different colors. Her wings were pure gold."

Sherry was stunned. She had not told anyone except Charlie about her angel encounter. "Mom, the same angel appeared to me, too. I think she's your guardian angel. She's going to take care of you."

Sherry talked with her about Jesus every time they were together after that. On one visit Mom said, "I don't even know how to pray."

"I'll help you," promised Sherry. The next time they went to visit, Sherry took her a copy of the Lord's Prayer.

Another time she asked, "How could God love me when I never believed?"

Sherry said, "He's always been there loving you. You just didn't know it."

Other people in the family also witnessed to her. She lived nearly a year and a half after the diagnosis, much longer than expected.

"Mom was a believer when she died," said Sherry. "She died peacefully, with absolutely no pain. That kind of peace can only come from God."

Dear Heavenly Father, thank you for this story, reminding us that out of the darkest storm clouds, angels can come to comfort us when we are distraught, lift us up when we are weak, and reassure us that we are not fighting life's battles alone. Help us to remember that angels are actively involved in building your kingdom here on earth today. In the name of your son Jesus Christ we pray. Amen.

37

Angelic Pallbearers

"The time came when the beggar died and the angels carried him to Abraham's side."

LUKE 16:22

"Who are you going to ask to do my funeral?" asked Ron's ninety-five-year-old mother, Nedra. She wasn't even sick at the time of the conversation, but she was making plans for the future.

"I don't know," Ron said. "Who do you want to do your funeral?"

"I've outlived all my pastors. Why don't you do it?"

As difficult as it would be, Ron agreed to his mother's request. She passed away a few months later. He began his eulogy, "We are here to celebrate my mother's new and exciting adventure, because that's what Mom wanted it to be—a celebration."

Ron described his mother as a woman of great faith who suffered a lot of hardships in life. "She had polio as a young girl, which left her with one leg shorter than the other, but it never slowed her down much.

"She was orphaned at the age of twelve. An aunt and uncle wanted to adopt her, but she was never formally adopted. However, they gave her forty acres of land in the northeast part of the county. She and Dad spent their whole lives on that land, rearing three kids and scratching out a living. We never had much, but Mom was deliriously happy and thankful for what we did have. She always gave the Lord the credit for her blessings.

"We always went to church. Mom provided the religious leadership in the home in a quiet way. As a young man, I remember one cold winter morning when I came in the house from milking the cows and doing the chores. I walked past her bedroom door, which was opened just a crack. She was down on her knees, praying at the side of the bed. I will never forget that sight. Mom had total respect for and trust in the Lord."

A family friend named Paul attended Nedra's funeral. "It was a very moving service," he said. "You could just feel God's presence there. I sat five or six rows behind the family. As Ron talked so lovingly about his mother and her faith, I saw several angels hovering around the family, maybe half a dozen of them. They looked like we all envision angels—dressed in dazzling white with wings and humanlike faces.

"A few seconds later," continued Paul, "I saw a vision of Jesus, even more vivid than the angels. He was above the casket, with the thorn of crowns on his head. He was looking down on her with his arms open, as if he intended to take her in his arms.

"The visions passed after fifteen or twenty seconds, but I know without a doubt that Jesus and the angels were there."

Scripture affirms that believers "will receive a rich welcome into the eternal kingdom of our Lord and Savior Jesus Christ." (2 Peter 1:11)

Scripture also affirms that we will be accompanied by angels. Billy Graham in his book, *Angels: God's Secret Agents*, writes that God commissions angels to escort each believer to heaven. He cites the story of Lazarus the beggar in Luke 16:22: "When the beggar died, the angels carried him to Abraham's side."[1]

Billy Graham refers to these angels as "angelic pallbearers."

I heard a similar story about angelic pallbearers from a pastor who described her father's funeral. She said, "My mother was too ill to attend his funeral, so we videotaped the service for her. Later that day we went to the nursing home and played the videotape. We were astounded as we watched the service. A host of angels were in the sanctuary during the service."

Dear Heavenly Father, thank you for the promise that we will be escorted to heaven by angels and receive a rich welcome into the eternal kingdom with your son, our Lord and Savior Jesus Christ. In his name we pray. Amen.

---

1. Graham, Billy. *Angels: God's Secret Agents* (Nashville: W. Publishing Group, 1994) 7-8.

38

Angels Minister to the Dying

"Now I know without a doubt that the Lord sent his angel."
ACTS 12:11

A farmer named Lloyd was diagnosed with a rare form of leukemia and was given only hours to live. His daughter, Connie, said, "We were advised to get the family together at the hospital as soon as possible. They moved him from intensive care to a hospice room furnished with a sofa and chairs for people to relax. We have a large family, so we decided to take turns staying by Daddy's bedside around the clock so that two people would always be there. Daddy was in a coma-like state to keep him calmed down because of intense pain.

"At 3 AM my brother, Kent, and I were the only ones up. Daddy began coughing and had trouble breathing, so we called for help and gathered the rest of the family around the bedside. There were three nurses dressed in white at the foot of Daddy's bed.

"Daddy was a singer and his favorite hymn was 'How Great Thou Art.' It was his trademark song. I was holding him in my arms when I heard someone singing 'How Great Thou Art.' It took me several moments to realize that I was the one singing. It had to be the work of the Holy Spirit because I sang every word of three stanzas. I don't even know all those words from memory. The moment I finished that song, I said, 'Daddy, the farming is done. It's time to go home.' His heart stopped beating at exactly that moment.

"The Lord said to me, 'It's okay Connie.' I knew exactly where he was going. What a privilege it was to hold my father in my arms and usher him into the arms of the Lord."

On the way home later that day Connie and her sister, Pam, were talking. Connie asked, "Who were those three nurses dressed in white at the foot of the bed?"

Pam said, "There weren't any nurses dressed in white. They all wore burgundy or blue uniforms."

"But I saw them there, in white dresses like nurses used to wear. After Daddy's heart stopped beating, I laid him back down on the bed. When I looked up, they were gone."

The Bible teaches that angels can appear to us in the form of human beings. For example, in Acts 12 there is the story of Peter's miraculous escape from prison. A man appeared to him and led him out of prison. When the man disappeared, Peter said, "Now I know without a doubt that the Lord sent his angel." (Acts 12:11)

There is no doubt in Connie's mind that God sent angels in human form to minister to her dying father.

Dear Heavenly Father, thank you for the presence of angels in this world who minister to us in miraculous ways. And thank you especially for those times when you pull back the curtain between heaven and earth so that we can see the angels. In the name of your son Jesus Christ we pray. Amen.

39

Angels in the Midst of Tragedy

Are not all angels ministering spirits sent to serve those who will inherit salvation?

HEBREWS 1:14

Late on a Sunday morning in September, Roger and his thirty-eight-year-old daughter, Kristine, were on their way to the grocery store. They were traveling on a two-lane highway in rural Indiana when Roger inexplicably veered to the left of the centerline and hit a motor home head-on. Roger died at the scene and Kristine was trapped in the wreckage.

When emergency personnel arrived on the scene, Kristine was conscious, but they had trouble communicating with her. It took rescuers a few minutes to realize she was deaf. One of the policemen said that a woman walked up to the scene of the accident and asked if she could help.

"I know sign language," the woman said.

"I was so grateful for her help," said the officer. "I couldn't believe someone who knew sign language showed up on the scene."

The "Jaws of Life" had to be used on the mangled wreckage to free Kristine. She was Life Lined to a hospital forty miles away. They feared she could have a broken neck, a broken back, or serious internal injuries.

Then the emergency personnel had another problem: How would they contact the next of kin? They learned that Roger and Kristine lived alone, so there was no one at home to give them information. They went through Kristine's purse and found only one item with a name and phone number—a check for $50 to Kristine for her birthday from her brother, Mike, in California. Through the address on that check, authorities were able to contact the family.

Mike said, "Every year I send Kristine $50 in cash for her birthday, but this time I didn't have the cash so I wrote a check, something I've never done before. Kristine got that check in the mail on Saturday. Sunday morning when the accident occurred, that uncashed check was in Kristine's purse with my phone number on it."

Kristine spent several days in the hospital. She had lots of bumps and bruises, but no life-threatening injuries, only a broken arm. One of the witnesses said she couldn't see how anyone could have survived that horrific crash.

A few days later Kristine's aunt went to visit her and took a gift—a small ceramic angel. When Kristine opened it, she burst into sobs and kept signing, "I saw you! I saw you!" Through a sign language interpreter Kristine told her story.

"After the accident," she signed, "two angels came, one for me and one for my dad. They were beautiful, surrounded by intense bright light, with golden hair and big wings with feathers. One of the angels lifted me up out of the car, and we looked down at the wreckage. The angel asked me, 'Do you want to go with me or go back to the car?'

"Then, the heavens opened up. I saw my mother who had died six months ago and my sister who had died six years ago. My mother urged me to stay, and when I agreed, the angel placed me back in the car.

"At the same moment, the other angel was ministering to my dad. I saw my mother with the angel, and they took him up into heaven."

Angels were present throughout this tragedy, from the moment of impact when an angel lifted Kristine from the wreckage, to the time when an angel ministered to her dad and took him to heaven.

Is it possible that God also sent an angel who knew sign language?

Dear Heavenly Father, thank you that you made your presence known in such powerful ways to Kristine and her family. Angels are, indeed, ministering spirits sent to serve those who will inherit salvation. In the name of your son Jesus Christ we pray. Amen.

40

Angels: God's Secret Agents

Blessed is the man who finds wisdom,
the man who gains understanding.

PROVERBS 3:13

"Has God ever spoken to you through a child?"

That was the question in a Sunday evening Bible study on seeking God's wisdom. One of the main points was: Wise counsel may come from unlikely sources.

Angela, one of the women in the class, said, "I don't usually talk about this because it makes me cry, but I feel like I should share this with you. God used my two-year-old daughter, Lucy, to speak to me when I was grieving over my father's death.

"Several years before my father died, I purchased Billy Graham's book, *Angels: God's Secret Agents*. He talks about some of the realities of the Christian life, that there are angels in heaven, but Satan is also active in our world. In fact, Satan himself is a fallen angel. One section was on 'The Current Cult of the Demonic;' another was titled, 'The Reality and Power of Satan.'[1]

"It frightened me, so I immediately put that book down. I didn't want to read any more of it."

It was left unread on her bookshelf for years. Angela finally stuck it underneath her bed in the middle of a stack of books she wanted to get rid of.

Two weeks after Angela's father died, she was struggling with grief and asking God a lot of questions: What really happens when you die? What did my dad experience at the point of death?

Angela said, "I was very emotional and crying when Lucy walked up to me with that angel book in her hand."

"Mama, read!"

"Lucy, this book doesn't have any pictures. You don't want Mommy to read this to you."

Angela said, "I took that book in my hands, intending to put it back underneath my bed, but somehow I knew immediately God wanted me to look at it again. Since I already knew I didn't like the beginning of the book, I opened it toward the back. There was the answer to my prayers in a section called 'Christians at Death,' where I read these words:

> God surrounds death with the assurance of angelic help for believers. . . . Death for the Christian cuts the cord that holds us captive in this present evil world so that angels may transport believers to their heavenly inheritance.[2]

Billy Graham quotes Hebrews 1:14: "Are not all angels ministering spirits sent to serve those who will inherit salvation?"

It was a comforting answer to Angela's question about what happens at the time of death.

Angela said, "Maybe God sent an angel to guide Lucy to bring me that book! She dug it out from underneath my bed and handed it to me at precisely the moment I needed it."

> *Dear Heavenly Father, thank you for the unpredictable ways you provide for us in our grief. Answers to prayer can come from unlikely sources, even from a two-year-old child holding a book about angels. Help us to always have our eyes and hearts open to you. In the name of Jesus Christ we pray. Amen.*

---

1. Graham, Billy. *Angels: God's Secret Agents* (Nashville: W. Publishing Group, 1994) 7-8.

2. Ibid., 164.

41

The Music Box Angels

*For he will command his angels concerning you
to guard you in all your ways.*

PSALM 91:11

"I was helping an elderly friend of mine move into the assisted living section of a nursing home," said Dave. As always, when people are forced to downsize, she didn't have room for all her possessions. "Would you like this wind-up music box?" she asked.

"Sure," said Dave. "It was topped with three little angels playing different musical instruments. I took it home and set it on my bedroom dresser. I don't remember that I ever wound it, so I didn't even know what tune it played. I kept my socks and handkerchiefs in the top drawer of that dresser, so I opened and closed that drawer every day for the next four years.

"On August 25, when I closed that drawer, the music box started playing—just four notes . . . ding, ding, ding, ding. The message to me was unmistakable. My mother had died the day before on August 24. If any symbol could be associated with Mom, it was angels. She believed in angels and collected them. She probably had between two and three hundred angels in her house.

"During the next three days leading up to the funeral, the music box dinged three more times as I opened and closed that drawer. That's when I wound it up to see what song it played. It was 'Hark! The Herald Angels Sing.'"

I attended the funeral for Dave's mother, where the angel theme was carried out. On the front of the funeral program was a picture of an angel, along with his mother's favorite Bible verse, Psalm 91:11: "For he will command his angels concerning you to guard you in all your ways." She also chose that verse as the epitaph on her tombstone.

The family chose different angels from her collection to display at the funeral. One was on the spray from the children covering the casket, another was in the bouquet from the grandchildren, and yet another in the flowers from the great-grandchildren. Figurines of angels were on display among the funeral bouquets. Some belonged to Dave's mother; others were from friends who knew her love of angels.

When Dave rose to say a few words about his mother, he carried a shoebox. He opened it and carefully unwrapped the music box and set it on the lectern as he told us about his mother's love of angels and that the music box had played four times since she had died. At the end of his remarks, he placed the music box on his mother's closed casket, and once again, there was a single ding from the music box.

Dave took the music box home and placed it back on his bedroom dresser. During the next day or two it dinged two more times. It has been silent now for months, just as it was silent for four years before her death.

Dear Heavenly Father, thank you for this gift of comfort to Dave at the passing of his mother. We are promised that angels will be present as we pass from this life to the next. Without a doubt, Dave's mother is enjoying eternal life with you in heaven, surrounded by a host of angels. In the name of Jesus Christ we pray. Amen.

SECTION SEVEN
PARTING GIFTS

42

On This Side of Heaven's Door

"As a mother comforts her child, so will I comfort you."

ISAIAH 66:13

"I had never been so close to someone dying," said Irene, "so the whole experience was new to me."

Irene's father was diagnosed with Stage 4 lung cancer. The next three months were a struggle as he went through the dying process.

"I prayed for healing at first," she admitted, "but then I had to face reality: My father was dying."

She pleaded, "God, what do I pray for now?"

God's answer was immediate and very clear: "Pray for peace for yourself and for your dad."

Near the end, Irene's whole family was at the hospital: two brothers, a sister, her mother, and several nieces and nephews.

"One of us stayed awake with him at all times," said Irene. "I was alone with Dad around 2 or 3 AM, seated in a chair at one side of his bed holding his hand. Suddenly I saw a vision of my grandmother who had passed away fifteen years ago. She appeared on the other side of the bed, leaning over her son, as if whispering to him, but I didn't hear a thing. She leaned so close that they may have been cheek to cheek, comforting him as she must have done when he was a child.

She never acknowledged me or the surroundings. It was just mother and son at that sacred moment.

"Grandma looked like she did when she died at age ninety-three with stunning wavy white hair," said Irene. "She was wearing a simple housedress and had her hands folded to her chest. The vision lasted only a few moments. I was the only one in the family who saw her.

"Dad passed away peacefully several hours later. I could feel God's arms holding me as he died, and I had the type of peace that can't be described, a peace that could only come from God."

Irene's perception of death changed at that moment. "Now I am no longer sad about dying or afraid to die—an amazing gift from God."

Irene knew she had seen her grandmother in that hospital room, but she had questions about it so she made an appointment with her pastor. "He gave me the most magnificent explanation," said Irene.

He said, "I think that at the point of death, the line between heaven and earth is so thin that sometimes we can see from one realm into the other, almost as if we are eavesdropping on something sacred. God gave you the gift of actually seeing your grandmother on this side of heaven."

His explanation reminded me of a statement from Billy Graham, "Only one thin veil separates our natural world from the spiritual world. That thin veil we call [physical] death."[1]

Irene talked to another pastor who affirmed what he said: "Sometimes God gives us extraordinary gifts like this at the death of a loved one. It was not an accident that you saw your grandmother. It was God's way of helping you cope with losing your father."

> *Dear Heavenly Father, thank you for the gift of peace that you granted Irene at her father's passing from this world to eternity, and thank you that his mother was there to usher him into your presence. In the name of Jesus Christ we pray. Amen.*

---

1. Graham, Billy. *Angels: God's Secret Agents* (Nashville: W. Publishing Group, 1994), 164.

43

Final Gifts: Communications of the Dying

> *Jesus said to his disciples, "I am going there to prepare a place for you... I will come back and take you to be with me."*
>
> JOHN 14:2-3

    I read an interesting book titled *Final Gifts: Understanding the Special Awareness, Needs, and Communications of the Dying*,[1] written by two hospice nurses, each with three decades of experience tending to the needs of the dying.

    Several common themes emerged. The most prevalent theme is being in the presence of someone who has already died, even interacting with them (talking, smiling, nodding). This never seems to upset or frighten the dying. On the contrary, they are more at peace when they know they will be in the presence of loved ones who have passed on.

    One of the stories came from a middle-aged man whose mother had a stroke, which left her in a coma for several weeks. Moments before she died, she awoke, broke into a beautiful smile, and reached for something unseen. She put her arms together and looked down joyfully, as if cradling a baby. She died in that posture with a look of happiness on her face.

The man explained that his mother's first baby had died moments after birth. She went on to have five other children; all survived and grew into adulthood. "We all knew Mother had lost a baby, but we never talked about it," he said. "From the look on her face, I know she died holding that baby again!"[2]

In my years of writing my newspaper column, I heard similar stories of people who were reunited with loved ones as they passed from this life to the next.

A woman named Elaine was at her dying mother's bedside. "At the end, Mom was completely paralyzed and needed constant attention. I witnessed a miracle of healing at the moment of death as she was able to sit up, look straight into my eyes, smile, and reach both of her hands up and say, 'It's okay. It's Paxton.'

"Paxton," Elaine explained, "was my 15-year-old son who died six years earlier. On her deathbed, my mother gave me the gift of peace, the assurance that she was in heaven with Paxton."

Stories like these are affirmed through the promises in the Bible. Paul said in his letter to the Romans, "The gift of God is eternal life" (Romans 6:23) Jesus himself said he was going to heaven to prepare a place for us and then he added, "I will come back and take you to be with me" (John 14:2-3). And one of the most often quoted verses from the Bible is the last line of Psalm 23 that we "will dwell in the house of the Lord forever."

Dear Lord, thank you for these stories of confirmation of eternal life. We believe the promises in your Word. In the name of Jesus Christ we pray. Amen.

---

1. Callanan, Maggie and Patricia Kelley. *Final Gifts: Understanding the Special Awareness, Needs, and Communications of the Dying* (New York: Bantam Books, 1997).

2. Ibid., p. 179.

44

A Child's Faith and Grandma's Last Goodbye

"Let the little children come unto me, for the kingdom of God belongs to such as these."

MARK 10:14

"Grandma's not going to live much longer," Linda explained to her two young sons, six and eight years old. "She will be going to heaven soon to be with Jesus."

Linda's mother had been ill for some time, so she carefully prepared her children for that moment.

"I was with her at the hospital on the morning she passed away," said Linda. "I was upset and crying as I drove to the grade school to break the news to the kids. My six-year-old son, Michael, was in his first-grade classroom.

"Honey, I wanted to let you know that Grandma passed away this morning."

He gave her a quizzical look. "Then why are you crying? If Grandma went to heaven to be with Jesus, isn't that a good thing?"

"Yes," Linda admitted. "That's a good thing."

"Then why are you crying?" he persisted.

"Because I will miss her."

"Okay, you can cry because you miss her. But you can't cry because she's in heaven. That's a good thing."

Linda said, "Michael was actually annoyed with me for being so upset!"

Six-year-old Michael had that simple, uncomplicated faith that we all long for. No wonder Jesus said, "Let the little children come unto me, for the kingdom of God belongs to such as these" (Mark 10:14).

When Michael got up the next morning for breakfast, he said to his mother very matter-of-factly: "Grandma came to see me last night."

"Really?" said Linda, trying to act nonchalant about his revelation.

"Yeah. She came to kiss me and tell me goodbye. She said she loved me."

"That was nice."

"Yeah, that was really nice."

Children accept the miraculous without question. They don't require an intellectual understanding. How does this happen? My pastor explained it this way: "Children are very connected spiritually, different from adults. Children are more open. They don't discount things the way we do. As we live longer in the world, that window of openness to spiritual happenings becomes smaller and smaller. Our human minds try to figure things out instead of just accepting these events as gifts from God."

Dear Heavenly Father, thank you for the complete, unquestioning faith of a child. Help us to be open to you with a child's simplicity and receptivity. In the name of Jesus Christ we pray. Amen.

45

Heaven through a Mother's Eyes

"Rejoice that your names are written in heaven."

LUKE 10:20

"My oldest cousin, Joann, was seventy-two years old," said Mike. "She was an exciting, fun person to be around and always very strong in her faith and in her church. She was a choir member for years and even directed the choir in a park where they wintered in Texas.

"In January Joann realized something was wrong. She was soon diagnosed with an aggressive type of cancer and began chemo and radiation, but after a week, she decided not to continue with the grueling treatments.

"The family notified me that she had gone into a hospice program and time was short. Five days later I got the call that she passed away."

On a Sunday afternoon, Mike sat with his cousins and other family members sharing memories of Joann. Her children said the last four or five days of her life, a number of times she described what she was seeing and hearing on the other side.

At one point Joann said, "Oh, my, look at the light over the hill. . . . There's Grandma Simpson. She's calling me!"

Mike said, "My Grandma Simpson died in 1974, more than

twenty-five years ago. Joann saw her and heard her calling to come to the other side."

At another point Joann shared, "The music is so beautiful. I've never heard music like that before."

Later on Joann saw her mother and had a conversation with her. "She said she's coming for me," she told her children.

Six hours before she died, Joann sat up on the bed, swung her legs over the side and shouted, "Look! They're all here for me! They're all here!" Those were her last words.

Through tears Mike said to his cousins, "What a wonderful gift—the opportunity to look into heaven through your mother's eyes. You were so blessed to be a part of that and to share that witness with us."

Mike said, "Nonbelievers would write off these experiences as reactions to strong drugs given to the dying to keep them out of pain, but as believers we know that this is total assurance that what we believe about heaven is true.

"The day of her funeral was truly a celebration. She's not in pain anymore, and we can all picture her holding court up there in heaven with the whole family. We will miss her, but we know she will be part of that group waiting on us when we get there."

Mike's story brought to mind the words to an old hymn by Fanny Crosby: "Blessed assurance, Jesus is mine! O what a foretaste of glory divine!"

Dear Heavenly Father, thank you for the promise of eternal life. We claim Jesus' words for believers in Luke 10:20, "Rejoice that your names are written in heaven." In the name of Jesus Christ we pray. Amen.

46

The Last Supper

*"I tell you, I will not drink of this fruit of the vine
from now on until that day when I drink it anew
with you in my Father's kingdom."*

MATTHEW 26:29

Mike's mother was in the hospital in the final stages of a long battle with cancer. Mike said, "She had been in a coma for four days with no response whatsoever. The immediate family gathered in her room—my father, my brother and his wife, and my wife, Sharon. We talked quietly, laughed about funny memories, and shed a few tears as we remembered the tender moments.

"Shortly after noon an elder from our church brought in Holy Communion. We all took the bread and ate it. Then we took the cup and drank it. As soon as I drank the cup, my mother opened her eyes, looked right at me and said, 'Where's mine?'

"Her eyes were the most radiant bright blue I had ever seen, almost as if a light were shining from behind her eyes. I took the cup, placed it to her lips, and she drank the cup. Then she closed her eyes and returned to her comatose state. Those were her last words. She never regained consciousness. She died three days later.

"What an honor it was for me to be able to serve my mother her final earthly Communion. It's a memory I shall always cherish."

How appropriate it was that they were sharing memories of their loved one at the time Communion was offered. The Lord's Supper is our way of remembering that Jesus died for our sins. In fact, Jesus commanded us, "Do this in remembrance of me."

The word "communion" means "a sense of sharing and fellowship, which arises out of a common bond." Holy Communion is a time of celebrating our bond with God and with other believers. Certainly, Jesus had a common bond with his disciples as they shared in what we now call The Last Supper. Their lives were intertwined for three years. They shared many meals together, but this one was different. Jesus used that Passover meal to prepare the disciples for his physical death and to remind them of the promise of eternal life. Jesus said in Matthew 26:29, "I tell you, I will not drink of this fruit of the vine from now on until that day when I drink it anew with you in my Father's kingdom."

As Mike's mother participated in her last supper with her earthly family, she could have used exactly the same words: "I will not drink of this fruit of the vine from now on until that day when I drink it anew with you in my Father's kingdom."

This last act was a beautiful affirmation of her belief in Jesus Christ as the Son of God, his sacrifice for us on the cross, and in the promise of eternal life.

Dear Heavenly Father, thank you for this beautiful parting gift to Mike and his family. This last supper was the beginning of a new life with you. In the name of Jesus Christ we pray. Amen.

47

A Time to Mourn and a Time to Dance

> *There is a time for everything, and a season for every activity under heaven: . . . a time to mourn and a time to dance.*
>
> ECCLESIASTES 3:1, 4

More than twenty years ago a friend of mine named Sharon was living in Washington D.C. working as an occupational therapist. Sharon said, "I became very good friends with one of my patients named Peggy, a stroke victim. I saw Peggy privately for years. The right side of her body was affected. Eventually, she was able to walk with a cane. Even though she couldn't attend church anymore, Peggy became more devout in her faith after her stroke. She lived alone in an apartment, but she wrote inspirational letters to friends and performed many small kindnesses for people

"When we adopted a little girl from Korea and named her Angela, Peggy gave her a very special gift: a wind-up music box with a dancing ballerina on top. Angela was already a toddler when we adopted her. She was enthralled with that dancing ballerina, to the point that she over cranked it, and it finally quit working.

"The music box sat in Angela's room for the next two years, until I was in the process of painting Angela's room, so I moved it to the dresser in my bedroom for safekeeping. Late one morning the music box that had been silent for over two years suddenly played a few notes. If I had been in any other room of the house, I would have missed it. It brought back good memories of Peggy.

"Two days later, one of Peggy's family members called to say that she had passed away. As we talked about the time of death, I knew without a doubt that the music box played at the exact time she died. It was her way of telling me that she was in heaven. The music box with the dancing ballerina never chimed again."

I had this story in my files for years. God reminded me of it when I attended a memorial service—a Celebration of Life—for a woman named Dorothy. She, too, had a long struggle with physical disability and needed assistance when walking.

When she was dying, a favorite nurse stayed at the bedside with the family all through the night. At her moment of death, the nurse said, "She's dancing in heaven!" Appropriately, the last song in the memorial service was "Lord of the Dance," where Jesus said, "They buried my body and they thought I'd gone, but I am the dance and I still go on. I'll live in you if you live in me. I am the Lord of the Dance, said he."

I thought again of the dancing ballerina music box. Maybe that final chime was Peggy's way of saying to Sharon, "I don't need that cane anymore. I have a perfect body now. I'm dancing in heaven with Jesus."

> *Dear Heavenly Father, we have the promise that in heaven "our lowly bodies will be like his [Jesus'] glorious body." (Philippians 2:21) We claim that promise, along with the assurance of eternal life with our Savior Jesus Christ, the Lord of the Dance. Amen!*

48

It's Just a Little Farther . . . It's Beautiful

The Lord made the heavens. Splendor and majesty are before him.

PSALM 96:5-6

I attended a memorial service for a woman named Dottie, whose son, John, reminisced about his mother, especially their wilderness trips. John said, "We had the privilege of going on three-generation canoe trips with Mother and Dad to places like Lake Superior. They always enjoyed themselves, but when you get into the rhythm of canoeing, there are long stretches of time doing nothing but paddling. Somewhat exasperated at one point, Mother said, 'How much farther?'

"How many times as kids had we asked her the same question? It was fun to turn the tables on her," said John.

"See that point way down there on the horizon?" I told her. "It's just around that point."

Some time later, the same question: "How much farther?" And the same answer: "See that point down there on the horizon? It's just around that point."

This conversation was repeated six or eight times before they reached their destination. "But it was worth the wait," said John. "It was beautiful."

That story became part of the family folklore as it was told again and again over the years.

Another memory John shared was about a different journey with his older brother, Ken, and his little sister, Debbie, in the Michigan wilderness. "I was the middle child, and Debbie was quite small at the time. Ken must have been in his teens because he was driving. We discovered a marvelous little hidden stream way back in the woods. When we got back, Mother and Dad were game to go see this magical place.

"As Ken drove, he said, 'It's just a little farther.' And Debbie's little voice from the back seat said, 'It's beautiful!' Every few minutes the same conversation was repeated: 'Just a little farther.' And Debbie's excited response: 'It's beautiful!'

"I think Mother wondered if that place really existed. It did exist. And it was beautiful."

That story, too, became part of the family folklore.

"Mother's last journey was the night she made that Grand Transition ahead of us all. I had a special time with her that evening. No, I wasn't here with her in Indiana. I was at home in Michigan. It was about 4:30 AM when Dad called and told us that she had passed on. Then Ken called and we had a nice talk, but I couldn't get back to sleep. I wasn't feeling heartsick. I was actually feeling celebratory for Mother that she had a peaceful passing, but I just couldn't sleep. I was up and down several times.

"About 6 AM in that 'netherworld' between wakefulness and sleep, that place where great things can happen, my eyes were closed when this wonderful, blue radiant light appeared."

John paused for a moment as he added, "Experiences like this are written about by sages and prophets down through the ages. I am not one of those by any means.

"This wonderful luminescent blue light came into my mind's eye. It was an almost overpowering feeling. I was in control, but I was not driving this experience. Somewhere deep inside of me came: 'Mother?' And then a very simple, one-word answer, loving and matter-of-fact like Mother always was: 'Yes.'

"That experience went on for a few minutes and then it passed.

I know what Mother was telling me: 'It's just a little farther . . . It's beautiful!'"

Yes, we are promised a glorious future: eternal life with our Lord and Savior Jesus Christ in heaven. And, yes, it's beautiful!

> *Thank you, dear Lord, for this parting gift, affirming once again the gift of eternal life with you. It is in your name that we pray.*
> *Amen.*

49

A Great Reunion in Heaven

"Whoever believes in Him shall not perish but have eternal life."
JOHN 3:15

"Mom," said Sherry, "who are you talking to?"

"Your Grandma, Grandpa, and Uncle Don," she said. "But close the door. Charlie will think I'm crazy."

Sherry's mother was nearly blind and dying when she moved in with Charlie and Sherry for the last six weeks of her life. She had frequent "imaginary" conversations with her deceased mom, dad, and brother, Don. Sherry didn't argue with her mother about it, but she didn't really believe her either. "I thought these hallucinations were from her medications or some kind of mental confusion."

One day Sherry's mother announced: "Uncle Don says to tell you he likes your new house, especially the music in your bathroom."

"Music in the bathroom?" asked Sherry.

"Yes, he says you have violins in your bathroom."

Sherry thought, *What on earth could she mean?* She walked into her bathroom and looked around. There was the answer: The wallpaper border next to the ceiling was filled with violins.

"Mom was nearly blind," Sherry said. "There is no way she could have seen that strip of wallpaper at the ceiling."

I again turned to the book *Final Gifts* written by two hospice nurses. In Chapter 7, "Being in the Presence of Someone Not Alive," they explain that this is the most prevalent theme they encounter with the dying.

"The timing varies," they state. "The experience can happen hours or days or sometimes weeks before the actual death. . . . They recognize someone significant from their lives. . . . There is often a sense of pleasure, even of joyful reunion, in seeing that person again. . . . Most accept these other presences without question."[1]

The last day of her life, Sherry's mother sat up in bed and announced: "I saw Jesus. Be happy for me because I know where I'm going."

This, too, is a common occurrence with the dying. People see angels or Jesus as they get close to death. It's never frightening to them; it's always comforting.

The last words Sherry's mother spoke were, "Grandma, Grandpa, and Uncle Don are coming for me at 5 PM."

As it got closer to 5 PM, Sherry's mother slipped into a coma. She died that evening. This phenomenon was confirmed by the *Final Gifts* authors, too, in Chapter 15, "Choosing a Time."[2] It's not unusual for the dying to know the time they will die and even announce it to others.

> *Dear Heavenly Father, thank you for these parting gifts from Sherry's mother. We don't always understand your workings in the world, but one thing we know without a doubt is that we will have a glorious reunion with you and our loved ones in heaven. In the name of Jesus Christ we pray. Amen.*

---

1. Callanan, *Final Gifts*, p. 83.

2. Callanan, *Final Gifts*, p. 197.

SECTION EIGHT

READY FOR HEAVEN

50

The Greeter

You will receive a rich welcome into the eternal kingdom of our Lord and Savior Jesus Christ.

2 PETER 1:11

My church, like most churches, is designed with a narthex, that area between the outside door and the entrance into the sanctuary. Normally on Sunday mornings, it's an area where the official greeters stand to welcome people to church. Then the official ushers escort people to their seats in the sanctuary.

On a Wednesday in October at 10:30 AM, I walked through the front doors of my church into the narthex. The official church greeters did not meet me inside the door this time. Instead, I was greeted by a long line of mourners waiting their turn to express condolences to the family of Bonnie Smith, a friend and fellow member of my church. Bonnie died of breast cancer, leaving her husband and two young boys.

As the line moved slowly toward her open casket, I caught a glimpse of something bright yellow. Only when I got closer did I realize that pinned to her suit was something she had worn many times before: her nametag that said, "Bonnie Smith, Greeter."

Bonnie had a great sense of humor. From her heavenly vantage point, she must have enjoyed greeting her friends and loved ones in this final way. She was buried with that nametag on, so it's my last memory of her earthly body. My image of Bonnie now is one of her standing at the door of heaven wearing that bright yellow nametag, greeting people with handshakes or hugs, and welcoming them gladly into the presence of God.

She fit the definition of the word "greeter" perfectly—a person who welcomes others gladly. Bonnie enjoyed fulfilling that role in our church. Her love for people and her warm spirit made her a natural at the job.

Bonnie was a person of great faith. Several times in the last two weeks of her life, she expressed how much she looked forward to meeting Jesus. She knew without a doubt that Jesus would greet her at the door as she passed from this life into the next and that she would be ushered into the presence of God. Without a doubt, she was ready for heaven.

Dear Heavenly Father, Thank you for Bonnie's life and powerful witness. We look forward to seeing Bonnie as a heavenly greeter, welcoming others into your eternal kingdom. In the name of Jesus Christ we pray. Amen.

51

In My Father's House Are Many Rooms

*"In my Father's house are many rooms; . . .
I am going there to prepare a place for you."*

JOHN 14:2

Kristine, a vibrant eighteen-year-old, was involved in all the normal activities of a senior in high school when she became critically ill. She was admitted to the hospital, and within a few days, she was diagnosed with an often-fatal disease.

Kristine's parents were devastated when doctors said, "There's nothing more we can do except keep her comfortable." They asked for help from the hospital staff to break the news to their daughter.

A woman named Donna is part of a hospital team that works with critically and terminally ill patients and their families. "When Kristine heard the prognosis," said Donna, "she was naturally quite upset, but when I went to see her later, her demeanor was completely changed. Kristine had in her hand a collection of swatches from a paint store, those little strips of various shades of color. She fanned them out like a deck of cards and said, 'Pick a color.'

"I didn't know what was going on," said Donna, "but I played along. I chose a bird's egg blue. Then Kristine explained: 'Since I'm going to heaven before you, I want to paint your room your favorite color.'

"Anytime a different person came into Kristine's room after that, she had them choose a color for their room in heaven."

Donna said, "I have worked with critically and terminally ill patients for years, but I was bowled over by the spiritual maturity of an eighteen-year-old who was so certain of her place in heaven. Kristine knew this world is just a passing-through place. It's not the final destination. She used those paint swatches as a tool to witness about eternal life and to help the people around her accept her physical death."

Kristine was a living witness to the promise in John 14:1-3 as Jesus tried to prepare his disciples for his impending death:

> "Do not let your hearts be troubled. Trust in God. Trust also in me. In my Father's house are many rooms. If it were not so, I would have told you. I am going there to prepare a place for you. And if I go and prepare a place for you, I will come back and take you to be with me that you also may be where I am."

When Kristine passed away, she continued to witness to people at the funeral because those paint swatches were in the casket with her. Kristine's story was repeated to everyone who passed by.

"As Christians, we have the certainty of eternal life," said Donna. "How wonderful it was for Kristine and her family to be able to frame death in such a beautiful way."

Dear Heavenly Father, thank you for the promise of eternal life. Help us to learn from Kristine's example of faith in your Word. In the name of Jesus Christ we pray. Amen.

52

I Know What Awaits Me

He was caught up into Paradise.

2 CORINTHIANS 12:4

A friend of mine named Dave had open-heart surgery on September 24, 2004. The surgery was very difficult and involved. In fact, the nationally known heart surgeon said it was the worst heart he had ever operated on.

Soon after the surgery, Dave shared with his family that he had died on the operating table. "I actually lifted out of my body and hovered above it, the most peaceful, yet exciting feeling I've ever had. I was surrounded with God's incredible peace, love, warmth, and light. Then a voice spoke to me very clearly: 'Would you like to go or stay?'

"I hesitated for a moment. It was a tough decision. It would have been much easier to give up the physical struggle and go. But then I said: 'I need to stay for my wife and three girls.'

"Calmly and peacefully I settled right back down into my body."

The anesthesiologist followed Dave out of surgery telling people: "This here is a miracle man!" He had witnessed a man who died on the operating table and came back to life.

Dave said, "The anesthesiologist stayed around for another shift on his own time to be there with me and share the experience. That was incredible.

"This experience confirmed for me that I am not afraid to die. I know what awaits me."

Dave waited more than two years to tell me this story. He said, "I am only now to the point where I am comfortable talking about this with a few people. It's not something I share lightly."

As I thought about Dave's experience, God showed me a passage in 2 Corinthians 12:2-4 about the apostle Paul describing his visions and revelations from the Lord. In my Bible this section is titled, "The Vision of Paradise." Paul writes as though he is describing another person:

> I know a man in Christ who fourteen years ago was caught up to the third heaven. Whether it was in the body or out of the body I do not know—God knows. . . And I know that this man—whether in the body or apart from the body I do not know, but God knows—was caught up to paradise.

According to a footnote in my Bible, the term "third heaven" refers to the highest heaven, the presence of God, in contrast to the sky and the starry heavens visible from Earth. And the term "paradise" is a place of blissful fellowship with God.

Like my friend, Dave, Paul did not fear death because he had already seen a glimpse of what was to come.

> *Dear Heavenly Father, thank you that as Christians we have no reason to fear death when we claim your promise of eternal life. We thank you for Paul's words, "We know that the one who raised the Lord Jesus from the dead will also raise us with Jesus." (2 Corinthians 4:14) In the name of Jesus Christ we pray. Amen.*

53

Don't Worry About Me

Jesus said, "Whoever loses his life for me will save it"
LUKE 9:24

Gene's forty-year-old brother, Brian, lived as a non-Christian most of his life. Gene explained, "Brian lived a rough life with no interest in church. He was pretty much a free spirit when it came to spiritual matters, but during the past year things changed. He began to search things out and decided it was time to get back in church. He was a changed man, as he developed a personal relationship with Jesus Christ."

Brian had a motorcycle he loved, but at the beginning of June 2008, Brian's mother said, "You need to get rid of that motorcycle. It's dangerous."

"Mom," said Brian, "if God decides to take my life on the motorcycle, it's okay with me. I've made everything right with God. Don't worry about me."

Brian lived in Columbus, Indiana, which was hit by a devastating flood on June 7. Brian went to check on his daughter's house nearby. By the time he got back to his trailer, the water was up to his knees. He lost his cars, his clothing, and everything in his home. All he had left were the clothes on his back and his motorcycle.

Brian's daughter and her husband flew home from Florida to check on the flood damage to their house. Brian worked with them until 1 AM. They were able to salvage some of her belongings. They headed back to his parents' home with Brian on his motorcycle, followed by his daughter and husband in their car. The weather turned cool, so Brian pulled off the road to put on a sweatshirt. He motioned for them to go around him. That was the last time they saw Brian alive.

They set out on a search for him, but in the chaos of flooded roads, it was hours before they found out what happened. Wildlife was so disrupted by the flood that Brian was struck by a deer as it fled the high waters. He died instantly.

"In just a few hours," said Gene, "Brian lost everything materially, but then he gained everything spiritually."

Brian died a pauper, but he was rich in the treasures of heaven.

Dear Heavenly Father, thank you for Brian's confidence of his place in heaven with you. He lost his worldly possessions, but then he gained everything as he entered into eternal life with you. In the name of Jesus Christ we pray. Amen.

54

Are You Homesick for Heaven?

*We would prefer to be away from the body
and at home with the Lord.*

2 CORINTHIANS 5:8

I have a friend who visits a woman at a local nursing home. When he asks her how she is doing, her response is always the same: "I'm homesick for heaven."

Perhaps she means she is tired of the physical body that eventually becomes a burden and she is ready to go on to something better. Physical death for Christians holds the promise of a new, perfect body in heaven where we will live eternally with our Lord and Savior Jesus Christ.

I have heard it said that we each have a hole in our heart that only God can fill. That hole can never be filled completely until we are in our eternal home with the Lord.

In a Billy Graham newspaper column titled, "We Were Not Created for This Life Alone," he wrote, "Every one of us senses that this life is not all, that there must be more. Where did this inner feeling come from? It came from God, who planted it in our hearts."[1]

My mother-in-law passed away when she was eighty-eight. She outlived her husband by two years, and all of her siblings and close friends had passed away. She was the last surviving member of her generation. She often said, "Holidays, birthdays, and anniversaries are hard because it brings back so many memories of loved ones who are gone." As a testament to her feelings, we found her tattered address book after she died with most of the names crossed out.

On the day she died, she was in the hospital being treated for a mild heart attack. She expected to come home that day; in fact, I was waiting for a phone call from the doctor telling me she was released. Instead, I got the unexpected phone call that she died suddenly.

Our family went to the hospital and gathered around her bed. The nurse, who was with her when she died, told us her last words were these: "My husband died two years ago. I'm so lonesome and tired. I'm ready to go home."

She didn't say it in so many words, but she, too, was homesick for heaven.

The apostle Paul in 2 Corinthians 5:1-8 wrote about our heavenly dwelling place:

> Now we know that if the earthly tent [physical body] we live in is destroyed, we have a building from God, an eternal house in heaven, not built by human hands. Meanwhile we groan, longing to be clothed with our heavenly dwelling.... We would prefer to be away from the body and at home with the Lord.

Dear Heavenly Father, you designed us to be homesick for heaven. We will never be completely at peace until we share eternal life with you. In the name of Jesus Christ we pray. Amen.

---

1. Graham, Billy. *The Indianapolis Star*, "We Were Not Created for This Life Alone." May 31, 2008, D4.

55

What Will It Be Like When I Die?

"Do not let your hearts be troubled...."

JOHN 14:1

As a young boy lay dying, he asked his mother, "Mommy, what will it be like when I die?"

She thought she had carefully prepared her son for death. She told him about Jesus, about living in heaven with a perfect body, and that he wouldn't be sick anymore. She was certain he had no fear of dying, but he wanted an explanation of what would happen at the exact moment of death.

After carefully considering her words, she answered in a way a child could understand: "Do you remember the times we drove to Grandma's house on Sundays to visit and sometimes we didn't get home until after your bedtime? You fell sound asleep in the back seat of the car. When we got home, Daddy scooped you up and carried you to your bed, tucked you in, and gave you a goodnight kiss. You didn't remember any of that. The next morning you woke up in your nice, warm bed. That's what it will be like when you die. You will fall into a deep sleep and then your Father in heaven will scoop you up and take you into heaven, a warm wonderful place where there is no more illness and you will have a perfect body."

The little boy smiled at his mother and fell into a coma. He soon passed peacefully from this life to the next.

As I was writing this story, God reminded me of another story with a similar question about what it will be like when you die. It must have happened some years ago, because it was about a doctor who was making a house call to a dying man. As the doctor said goodbye and began to open the bedroom door, the man said, "Doctor, I'm afraid to die. Tell me what lies on the other side."

Very quietly, the doctor said, "I don't know."

"You, a Christian man, don't know what's on the other side?"

As the doctor held the handle of the bedroom door, on the other side came a sound of scratching and whining. As the doctor opened the door, his faithful dog sprang into the room and leaped on him with an eager show of gladness. Turning to the patient, the doctor said, "Did you notice my dog? He's never been in this room before. He didn't know what was inside. He knew nothing except that his master was here, and when the door opened, he sprang in without fear. I know little of what is on the other side of death, but I do know one thing: My Master is there, and that is enough. When the door opens, I shall pass through with no fear, but with gladness."

When I finished writing this story and got ready to send it to the newspaper, I opened my e-mail and found a message titled, "What a Wonderful Way to Explain It." I clicked on it and couldn't believe my eyes. It was the same story about the doctor and the dying man's question: What lies on the other side?

Thank you, Lord, for confirming your perfect timing for this story.

> *Dear Heavenly Father, we don't know the details of what we will see on the other side, but we do know that you will be there, welcoming us with open arms. That's all we need to know. In the name of Jesus Christ we pray. Amen.*

56

I'm Not Afraid to Die

The peace of God, which transcends all understanding, will guard your hearts and your minds in Christ Jesus.

PHILIPPIANS 4:7

Dow had not felt well for several days. As the morning progressed, he knew there was something drastically wrong with his body. He called his doctor's office and was told to go to the emergency room immediately. Instead of calling an ambulance, he got in his car to drive himself there. The hospital was only a couple of miles away. But about a quarter of a mile down the road, he knew he was about to pass out. He was able to pull into the driveway of a neighbor, but he was too weak to get out of the car.

Dow said, "God was definitely looking out for me, because my neighbor was standing at the only window in the house where she could see the driveway. She came running out to see what was wrong. "I need to get to the emergency room," he said.

A few minutes after they arrived at the hospital, doctors told him, "You're having a heart attack." He was in and out of consciousness, but he said, "I remember dreaming that there was a brilliant white wall very close to me. I was shown a tiny glimpse of what was on the other side, and the most incredible feeling of peace came over me at that moment, a peace that I can't even describe."

He was stabilized and transferred by ambulance to a larger hospital where they performed an angioplasty. Dow said, "During the procedure, I realized that I could die. I remember thinking that I wanted to see that tunnel of white light that people talk about. As I looked beyond the surgeon, the wall in the room faded away. I could see to infinity. I saw freshly plowed fields with furrows running diagonally and very soothing, rolling ocean waves. I saw the tops of clouds with the sun shining on them, as if I were above the clouds. I saw all of these things simultaneously, yet separately, as if time and distance had no meaning. All the images had color, but not colors I can describe with words.

"I was filled with that incredible feeling of peace again, as the Holy Spirit reminded me of the verse about the peace of God that transcends all understanding (Philippians 4:7). The Holy Spirit assured me, 'You're not going to die.' The message could not have been plainer."

Dow was awake as two nurses wheeled him from the operating room into the Cardiac Care Unit. One of them said, "You're the calmest person we've had in there in a long time."

After the ordeal was over, people said to Dow, "I'll bet you were scared."

He answered, "No, I was not scared. God gave me the gift of peace, and I was assured by the Holy Spirit that I would not die. Besides, I know exactly where I'm going when I die. I've had a glimpse of heaven. I have no fear of death because I know I will spend eternity with my Lord and Savior Jesus Christ."

> *Dear Heavenly Father, thank you for the peace that surpasses all understanding and for the promise of eternal life. We look forward to spending eternity with you. In the name of Jesus Christ we pray. Amen.*

SECTION NINE

CALLED TO COMFORT OTHERS

57

Pray To Be Used and Then Obey

*We know that we have come to know him
if we obey his commands.*

1 JOHN 2:3

"God, please arrange for me to sit next to the person you want," I prayed as I left home to attend a women's luncheon. "Guide our conversation and help me recognize where you are working."

My daughter said, "Mom, God loves to answer prayers like that! It's exciting to see what will happen." I left home with a feeling of expectancy.

When I arrived at the luncheon, I sat with a group of women within earshot of four or five people. It was a nice luncheon, but at no point did I see God working. As I was ready to leave, a friend from the other side of the room sat next to me to chat. Still, nothing in our conversation caught my attention. As she rose to leave, she said, "I'm on my way to visit Elaine."

That was it. God spoke through my friend as clearly as if he were the one sitting next to me.

"I'll go with you," I said.

God had been urging me for days to visit Elaine in the hospital.

She was terminally ill, but I had hesitated to visit her. This was his way of getting me to obey. God gave me the gift of a friend to go with me.

We visited Elaine that afternoon, and we were the ones most blessed. It's amazing how God leads us to people who need our presence and our prayers, and then he uses those people to bless us and teach us about love and compassion.

I haven't had a lot of experience visiting people who are dying. Sometimes instead of relying on God to give me the words, I worry that I will say the wrong thing, or worse yet, that there will be long periods of uncomfortable silence.

A hospital chaplain gave me some advice about that. When he visits patients, one of his biggest obstacles is to convince them that sitting together in silence can be a good thing. Sometimes he says to the patient, "Talking takes energy. I'm not here for you to entertain me with conversation. Do you mind if I just sit here and pray for you in silence?"

He said, "I think people appreciate that."

When Jesus died, he sent the Holy Spirit to live within us. Now he is the one who calls us to visit the sick and the dying. He is also the one who gives us the right words or simply instructs us to sit in silence.

> *Dear Lord, help us to pray to be used by you, and then to watch and wait expectantly for an answer. After you have shown us what you want us to do, then give us the faith to obey, knowing that you will guide us every step of the way. In the name of Jesus Christ we pray. Amen.*

58

One Small Act of Kindness

"Now that I have washed your feet, you also should wash one another's feet. I have set you an example that you should do as I have done for you."

JOHN 13:14-15

I had lunch with a friend of mine named Mary. We talked about a mutual friend who died and the grief process the family goes through. Mary said, "One of the hardest things I had to do after my husband died was to go to church by myself for the first time. Now when a friend loses her husband, I call to make sure she has someone to go to church with, especially the first time."

Mary has used that painful memory of her experience and turned it into an act of kindness to other widows.

"Anything that you used to do as a couple is difficult to do alone. My husband and I loved to play golf. Playing for the first time without him was almost more than I could bear. I got into my golf cart all by myself and just sobbed as I went from one hole to another. A foursome of men was playing behind me. About halfway through the course one of them, a friend named Jim, walked over to say hello. When he saw how distraught I was, he said, 'Mary, I'll play with you.' He put his clubs in the back of my cart, and we finished the course together. Wasn't that a kind thing for him to do?"

Mary couldn't recall any other words Jim said to her. All she remembers is his one small act of kindness. His actions spoke louder than his words.

The astounding thing about this story is that Mary will be ninety-three years old next month. Her husband died when she was sixty-three—thirty years ago—and she still remembers that one small act of kindness.

As I wrote this story, God reminded me of an article I had read years ago about a young father who died, leaving a widow and several small children. A friend of the family went to the home to pay his condolences. He felt the need to help in some way, but he was at a loss as to what to do. Then he spotted a worn, scuffed pair of brown shoes that belonged to one of the little girls. He whispered something to the oldest boy, and then the two of them disappeared for a few moments. Without saying a word, the friend returned to the living room with a rag and a small can of shoe polish. He sat cross-legged in the middle of the floor and began to apply brown polish to those worn shoes while the boy searched the house for the other children's shoes. The man buffed those shoes until he could see his reflection in them. He completed this same, loving ritual with each shoe until he had a row of them lined up at the front door. Those children attended their daddy's funeral with shined shoes. The young widow said it was one of her most precious memories of one small act of kindness in a sea of despair.

That friend was being Jesus to a grieving family, making himself a servant in this loving, humble way. Can't you picture Jesus doing something like that? I couldn't escape the comparison between this story and the story in the Gospel of John when Jesus washed the feet of his disciples. Usually a servant performed that task. When Jesus took on the role of a servant, the disciples were uncomfortable with that, but Jesus used that occasion to teach about love, kindness, and selfless service to one another.

> *Dear Heavenly Father, Jesus gave us the perfect example of serving one another in love. Help us to remember that Jesus has no other hands and feet but ours. Help us to look for ways to express our love for Jesus through small acts of kindness, especially during times of grief. In the name of Jesus Christ we pray. Amen.*

59

God Is Faithful When We Obey

Moses said to the Lord, "I am not eloquent . . . I am slow of speech and slow of tongue" . . . and the Lord said, "Is not Aaron the Levite your brother? I know that he can speak well. And look, he is coming out to meet you."

EXODUS 4:10, 14

"Please don't ask me to go see her, God. I don't know what to say to a person who is terminally ill," I prayed. "I've never been around someone who is dying."

Have you ever argued with God? That's what I was doing when Bonnie, a friend from my church, was in the local hospital dying of cancer. I knew I should go visit her, and God kept nudging me to do so, but each time I resisted.

I would feel so much more comfortable if someone else could go with me, I thought.

The Holy Spirit immediately quickened me with the names of two other women in my church: Lu and Debbie. *They will know what to say and how to pray with Bonnie.* I started for the phone to call them, but the Lord assured me that I didn't need to call my friends, that he would be with me. So I mustered up my courage and drove to the hospital by myself, praying all the way that God would give me the right words. I stepped out of my car in the parking lot, turned around to head for the front door, and there was Debbie just stepping out of her car.

"Are you here to see Bonnie?" I asked.

"Yes," said Debbie. "In fact, I almost called you to come with me because I didn't want to come by myself."

"I had the same experience. God brought your name to mind, but I didn't end up calling you."

As we both headed toward the hospital door, who do you suppose drove into the parking lot? You guessed it—Lu!

All three of us knew we had just witnessed a little miracle. Isn't God good? He arranged for all three of us to arrive at the hospital at exactly the same moment so we could visit Bonnie together. We could not have choreographed the timing any better if we had planned it. We visited Bonnie, and God gave us the right words. It was the last time we saw her. She died a few days later. We were overwhelmingly thankful we obeyed.

The Bible story that came to mind with this incident is in chapters 3 and 4 in the Book of Exodus where God appeared to Moses in the burning bush. God wanted Moses to go to Pharaoh and tell him to let His people go:

> "O my Lord," Moses pleaded, "I am not eloquent. I am slow of speech and slow of tongue. Please send whomever else you may send."
>
> "Is not Aaron the Levite your brother?" asked the Lord. "I know that he can speak well."
>
> At the moment the Lord spoke Aaron's name, the Lord said, "Look, Aaron is coming to meet you now" (Exodus 4:13-14).

God arranged for Aaron to be there at exactly the time he was needed. Aaron accompanied Moses and became his spokesman for God.

> *Dear Lord, thank you that your people have ears to hear and then obey your commands. And thank you for arranging the right people at the right time to enable us to do what you have called us to do. You are an awesome God! In the name of Jesus Christ we pray.*
> *Amen.*

60

Called to Be Part of God's Buddy System

He has sent me to bind up the brokenhearted.

ISAIAH 61:1

"Words can hardly express our thanks for the many precious ways you have come alongside us in our journey through the Valley of the Shadow."

Those words began a letter marking the one-year anniversary of the death of a twenty-five-year-old medical missionary in Nigeria named Brianna (Bri). She died in a tragic road accident when a truck swerved into their lane. Bri, along with seven others on their mission team, died in that accident.

The letter continued: "Even as waves of grief continue to come upon us, we are tenderly comforted and strengthened by God's presence and by the compassion of his people. We have been powerfully upheld by your prayers and God's Word. Even though Bri's final sunset came far too soon for those of us who loved her so dearly, we are marveling at the brightness of her light still shining as friends and strangers hear of her amazing zeal and passion to honor and serve the Lord as a medical missionary, even when it cost her everything."

The letter from Bri's family ends with a story from Sheila Walsh, a speaker for Women of Faith, who told listeners about an insight she gained after she received a medical treatment for broken bones in her foot. The nurse told her that they bind the broken toe to the one that is whole so that it can support the broken bone until it is healed.

This treatment is called the "buddy system."

"Our hearts are broken," the letter continues, "and we desperately need God's 'buddy system.' Thank you for binding your hearts to ours through one of life's most painful times and supporting us until the healing takes place. One day, as with Bri, we will enter a glorious sunrise in heaven and meet the Lord face to face. 'He will wipe every tear from our eyes and there will be no more death or mourning or crying or pain.' (Revelation 21:4) Until then, we thank God for surrounding us with buddies to pray for us and support us through the days ahead! We love you!"

> *Dear Heavenly Father, as part of the Body of Christ, we are meant to be gifts of love and encouragement to one another. Show us someone who is in desperate need of your "buddy system." Guide and direct us to stand alongside them until they can once again stand on their own. As the prophet Isaiah said, "He has sent me to bind up the brokenhearted." (Isaiah 61:1) In the name of Jesus Christ we pray. Amen.*

61

Show Each Other Your Wounds

When the disciples were together, . . . Jesus came and stood among them . . . and he showed them his hands and side.

JOHN 20:19-20

Is the Kingdom of God strengthened when we share our wounds with one another?

If we follow the example of Jesus, the answer is yes. John 20:19-20 describes Jesus' appearance to the disciples the day after his crucifixion. They were together with the doors locked for fear of the Jews. Jesus came and stood among them and said, "Peace be with you!" Then Jesus showed them his pierced hands and side.

Isn't it interesting that the first thing Jesus did was to show them his wounds?

My husband and I had a friend who was going through a very difficult time of grief after the death of his wife. He isolated himself from others and dropped out of his normal activities. We were at a loss as to how to help him. Should we visit him, talk to him on the phone, send a note? Or should we respect his privacy and not contact him at all for a period of time? I prayed for God to give us an answer.

Immediately after I said that prayer, God led me to one of my devotional books called *The Experience: Day by Day with God* by Henry

Blackaby. The lesson for that day was titled, "Carrying Burdens" and was based on Galatians 6:2, "Carry each other's burdens, and in this way you will fulfill the law of Christ." He wrote:

> When someone we know is struggling under a heavy weight, we can do one of three things: pretend not to notice, criticize the person, or offer to help carry the load. You may think their burdens are none of your business: they have their problems, you have yours. But Paul says helping them is not only your business; it's your obligation. You can ease their load by showing love, acceptance, and encouragement.[1]

Without a doubt, this was an answer to prayer. We went to visit our friend and offered listening ears and prayer. Sometimes those are the best gifts of all. Yes, we should show each other our wounds, make ourselves vulnerable, and share our struggles.

As I was finishing this story, my husband called me from work with the perfect quote from a daily calendar on his desk. Elbert Hubbard wrote, "God will not look you over for medals, degrees, or diplomas, but for scars."

I would add: He will also look at how you responded to other people's scars. Did you respond with love and compassion?

We all have our own personal battles, but somehow the wounds are made easier to bear when they are shared with Christian friends. It's a great joy and an unparalleled privilege to stand alongside someone who is heavyhearted and help lift the burden.

> *Dear Heavenly Father, Help us to follow the example of Jesus and show each other our wounds. There are so many hurting and grieving people in this world. Help us to reach out to them in love and compassion. In the name of Jesus Christ we pray. Amen.*

---

1. Blackaby, Henry. *The Experience: Day by Day with God* (Nashville: Broadman & Holman Publishers, 1999), 337.

62

We Are Bound Together By Jesus Christ

A cord of three strands is not quickly broken.

ECCLESIASTES 4:12

In a Sunday evening class at my church, we studied a lesson called, "What About the Church?" I learned several things. First, the Greek word for "church" means "a gathering of people." The word "religion" comes from a Latin word that means "to bind together." So, a definition of the Christian church could be: "A gathering of people bound together by their belief in Jesus Christ."

But this definition does not do justice to the idea of a faith community supporting us in the good times and especially in the bad times. People who say they can be Christians without attending church are missing one of God's greatest blessings: the fellowship and support of our brothers and sisters in Christ. When people are bundled together into a community of faith, we are stronger. Ecclesiastes 4:12 expresses this beautifully: "A cord of three strands is not quickly broken." We draw strength for the journey from one another, and our lives are enriched far beyond what we could discover on our own.

Perhaps to understand this fully, you must experience that outpouring of love and support from your church family during times of illness, tragedy, or death. My husband and I experienced this type of love from our church family when his mother passed away suddenly a week before Christmas. You can't put into words what it means to receive a sympathy card with that simple message: "We are praying for you." Or to receive a phone call: "We are so sorry for your loss."

We also discovered that sometimes what we need is God with skin on—hugs from family and friends. After all, Christ has no other arms but ours.

A good friend just passed the anniversary of the death of a loved one, which brought on renewed despair and depression. She said, "I can't tell you how much it meant to me to receive 'Thinking of You' cards from my church family on that anniversary. When you know people are praying for you, it is somehow easier to bear. In fact, there have been times when I suffered from depression that suddenly lifted. I discovered later that at that very moment, someone in my church family was praying for me."

Another woman told me that she belongs to a weekly prayer group that meets for lunch. They share each other's joys and burdens. She experienced one of life's most devastating blows: the death of her only child. The grief is sometimes more than she can bear. On her son's birthday, she was too distraught to go to work. She felt a heavy burden of grief all morning, but then the burden suddenly lifted. Her whole attitude changed to one of peace. She looked at her watch. It was exactly one o'clock, the time when her sisters in Christ always pray for each other at the end of their meeting. She knew they were praying for her at that moment.

Repeatedly I have heard similar sentiments: "I don't know how I could have managed without the loving support of my church family. The grief would have been more than I could have borne."

We are bound together by our love for each other and by our belief in Jesus Christ.

Dear Heavenly Father, thank you for the gift of the church, for our faithful brothers and sisters in Christ who laugh with us during times of joy and cry with us during times of grief and despair. Use us as your hands and feet so we can draw strength and support from each other. It is in the name of Jesus that we pray. Amen.

SECTION TEN

CALLED TO WITNESS

63

A Joyful Witness for Christ

Whatever happens, conduct yourselves in a manner worthy of the gospel of Christ . . . Your attitude should be the same as that of Christ Jesus.

PHILIPPIANS 1:27; 2:5

It was a snowy February morning as I prepared to attend a funeral for a long-time member of our church, named Helen. During my morning prayer time, God brought to mind a story about Helen.

Several months earlier, Helen had sat next to me in church. Something in the service that day must have spoken to her because she turned to me at the end of the service and said, "I don't know how to witness to people. How do you witness to people? I just don't know how to do that."

I was speechless because I considered Helen one of the most powerful witnesses for Christ I have ever known, not through her words, but by the way she lived.

I developed a close relationship with Helen a year before she died. We were both undergoing chemotherapy for cancer. There were times when we sat side by side for our treatments in the oncology department at the local hospital, so we had a lot of time to talk. I was shocked when she told me she had been battling cancer for ten years! She always had a smile on her face, and she was so pleasant to be around, you would have thought we were on a social outing. That kind of response to adversity is contagious. She was a wonderful inspiration to me.

Helen reminded me of Paul's example of joy in the midst of adversity as he wrote from a prison cell to the church at Philippi. My Bible says that the theme of the book of Philippians is "The joy of knowing Jesus."

Like Paul, Helen was a joyful Christian, filled with the kind of joy that comes from living in the presence of God every minute of every hour of every day. I never heard her complain or speak negatively of anyone or anything. In short, she was Christlike. She was a living reminder that if we claim to be followers of Jesus Christ, then we must strive to live as he lived.

Dear Heavenly Father, Thank you for Helen's powerful witness in the face of adversity. We look forward to seeing her smiling face in heaven with you. In the name of Jesus Christ we pray. Amen.

64

The Privilege of Witnessing for Christ

God has given me the wonderful privilege of telling everyone about this plan of his; and he has given me his power and special ability to do it well.

EPHESIANS 3:7

Can you think of a time in your life when you knew without a doubt that you brought someone to Jesus Christ?

That question was asked in our adult Sunday school class. Wini immediately raised her hand. "Yes," she said. "I brought my sixteen-year-old sister to Christ. It happened in 1944."

She began to weep. "I still can't talk about it today without crying. I was twenty-two years old and had recently graduated from nursing school. My sister, Mary Jean, became ill, and after a few days, she had great difficulty breathing. We knew something was terribly wrong. We called an ambulance to take her to the hospital, and I rode with her in the ambulance. I think Mary Jean knew she would not be coming back home. She looked out the window of the ambulance at the house as we drove away, and I could tell by the look on her face that she knew she was dying."

Mary Jean was diagnosed with the worst kind of polio, the type that attacks the lungs. During the 1940s and 50s people lived in deadly fear of polio. They immediately put Mary Jean in an iron lung, a large metal cylinder that enclosed her entire body except her head. It acted like a respirator and kept her breathing.

"There were holes in the side of it so I could reach in and touch her and care for her," explained Wini. "The iron lung was pretty much a death sentence. I don't know anyone who survived it. Three other young people in the area were stricken at the same time. They were all on iron lungs in the same hospital and none of them survived."

Wini took time off from her nursing job to stay at Mary Jean's bedside and care for her. At one point, they thought she was getting better, so they took her off the iron lung and put her on another machine where she could have freer movement of her arms and legs. It was during that time that Mary Jean said, "Wini, I don't believe I know Jesus. I don't want to die without knowing him."

"Honey," said Wini, "all you have to do is pray and he will save you right this minute." They prayed the prayer of salvation, and Mary Jean gave her heart to the Lord.

Wini said, "It wasn't five minutes later that she took a turn for the worse, and they had to put her back in the iron lung. I called my folks, and they came to the hospital right away. She died a few hours later. Mary Jean lived only two weeks from the time she was stricken, but she died with a smile on her face. I know she saw Jesus.

"I feel honored that Mary Jean asked me to lead her to the Lord. We are commanded to lead people to Christ, but how many of us have the privilege of knowing without a doubt that God used us in that way?

"And another miracle happened as a result of her salvation. My father never went to church with the rest of the family, but after Mary Jean died, he began going to church. Mary Jean's death eventually led my dad to the Lord, too."

> *Dear God, thank you that you give us opportunities to witness for you, and along with those opportunities, you give us the ability, courage, and power to do it well. We are so privileged to be your servants. Many times we don't see the fruit of our labors, so we thank you for Wini's story where we can see not only Mary Jean's salvation but also her father's. In the name of Jesus Christ we pray. Amen.*

65

The Miracle of Salvation

If you confess with your mouth the Lord Jesus and believe in your heart that God has raised Him from the dead, you will be saved.

ROMANS 10:9

"We're not sure Dad's going to make it this time," Linda said to her family.

Linda's father had been in the cardiac intensive care unit for ten days. He was dying of congestive heart failure. The most recent crisis was that his kidneys had stopped working. Now he was on dialysis.

Linda said, "I had a crushing burden to witness to Dad before he died. He wasn't a believer, and I didn't think I had done everything I could for his salvation. I went to see him early in the morning so other visitors wouldn't be there. Another man was moved into his room overnight, and a curtain was pulled between their beds.

"I prayed for Dad and told him how much God loved him and that God wanted to receive him."

Linda did not receive assurance of her dad's salvation. "But I felt at peace about it," she said. "I told him what I felt God wanted me to tell him. The Great Banquet is prepared for everyone, but sometimes they turn it down."

Linda was referring to the story in Luke 14. The Great Banquet signifies the kingdom of heaven. Everyone is invited, but sometimes people make all kinds of excuses for not accepting the invitation.

As Linda went in and out of her dad's room during the day, she could see that the man in the next bed was dying. Joey was only forty-two years old. Toward evening, Joey's mother was there with him.

"Mother," said Joey, "will you please go to the lady sitting in the chair on the other side of the curtain? I want to talk to her."

Joey said to Linda, "I overheard you praying with your dad. Will you pray for me? I want to receive Jesus into my life."

Linda led him in the prayer of salvation. "It was so beautiful," she said. "I could see that he had a sense of peace after he accepted Christ." Joey died later that night.

"I thought it was my dad who was supposed to receive salvation that day, but it was Joey. My dad and Joey shared that room for only one night, but it was long enough for this miracle of salvation. Dad got better and was able to go home from the hospital, something we never expected. Now he attends church with us."

The following Sunday Linda was led to share this story with her congregation. A woman came up to Linda after the service with tears running down her face. "Thank you for being faithful," she said. "Joey was my cousin. I'm so thankful the Lord sent you to him."

Many people think that salvation is a complicated process. It is not. If you believe in your heart and confess with your mouth that Christ is the risen Lord, you will be saved.

Dear God, thank you for this miracle you arranged so that Joey could spend eternity with you. Remind us often that witnessing to people about their salvation is the most important thing we will ever do. It's a life or death matter. Help us to be bold in telling the Good News of Jesus Christ. It is in his name we pray. Amen.

66

Always Be Prepared to Share the Good News

Always be prepared to give an answer to everyone who asks you to give the reason for the hope that you have.

1 PETER 3:15

Some of the best sermons are preached at funerals. That was the case with Charlie, an extraordinary man who personally brought hundreds of people to Christ in his lifetime.

No, Charlie was not a minister of the gospel in the formal sense of the word. He did not have a seminary education. He didn't pastor his own church. But he demonstrated the concept of the priesthood of all believers, that we are all called to be priests to one another. He literally made the whole world his church.

Charlie had a passion for the Great Commission where Jesus commanded his disciples: "Go into all the world and preach the good news to all creation" (Mark 16:15). From the moment of his conversion, Charlie understood that God was concerned about all people in all places, especially those who had never heard of him.

His heart was broken for the lost on his first trip to South America as a new Christian. He came home and took thirty people back to South America with him. It wasn't long before he felt called to trade the insurance business for the mission field. During the next thirty-eight years, he led nearly two hundred trips.

Charlie gave the term "frequent flyer" a whole new meaning. He logged 4.5 million miles on Eastern Airlines before it folded in 1991. His family found a log in Charlie's desk after he died, which recorded another 4.8 million miles with United Airlines, mostly since 1988. He traveled a grand total of about 10 million miles.

He never "retired" from the ministry. He traveled an average of more than two hundred days per year. In the last year of his life, he took people to China twice. In his final month, he took a group to India, logging 25 thousand air miles in twenty-five days. God used him powerfully until his last day on earth.

His son-in-law, Jack, worked with Charlie for many years in ministry. He said, "It has been fascinating for me to watch how God guided Charlie to the right place at the right time or guided the right people to him. Nothing demonstrated this more than how often God guided searching people to the seat next to him on an airplane."

When asked his secret to sharing Christ so successfully with so many, he quickly responded: "I pray before I ever board a plane. I ask the Lord not to waste his time by sitting me by someone who isn't ready to hear the Good News. I board the plane as soon as possible and then watch the people coming down the aisle. I can usually guess which one will be sitting next to me—the one with the hopeless look on his or her face. Sure enough, that person plops down right next to me and I begin telling him or her about Christ."

That was Charlie's secret: He was so successful in sharing the gospel because he constantly prayed that God would give him the opportunity. And he was always prepared. He never went anywhere without his Bible. He lived by the credo in 1 Peter 3:15: "Always be prepared to give an answer to everyone who asks you to give the reason for the hope that you have."

Nothing defined Charlie's life more than his passion to see people come to Jesus. Everything else he did was a subtext and a vehicle for this. We can learn much from a life like Charlie's.

One of the most powerful testimonies I ever witnessed at a funeral consisted of seven words written on the gift card in a funeral bouquet:

"Thank you for introducing me to Jesus." The card was unsigned. What will be said at your funeral? Will there be stories of how your Christian witness brought others to Christ?

Dear Heavenly Father, give us the passion to spread the Good News, and enable us always to be prepared to give the reason for the hope that we have. Thank you for the opportunities you give us to witness about your love, and open our eyes to searching people you send across our path. In the name of Jesus Christ we pray. Amen.

67

Never Too Old to Witness

"And you will be my witnesses . . . to the ends of the earth."
ACTS 1:8

"God, I don't get out in the public as much as I used to. Use me more to witness about my faith," prayed Pattie.

Pattie retired from her teaching job six years earlier and didn't feel she had enough opportunities to witness to people anymore.

She got a call one day from an insurance woman wanting to talk to her. The insurance representative and a colleague arrived at Pattie's house, but after a short conversation they discovered there was a misunderstanding. Pattie already had the long-term care insurance they were selling, so the visit was unnecessary.

In spite of the misunderstanding, they began a friendly conversation. Pattie told them about her ninety-three-year-old father who lived in Portland, Oregon, and the decision her family had to make for his long-term care.

"Daddy lived with my sister until it became impossible for him to navigate the stairs to his bedroom. Instead of a nursing home, we began looking for a private care home, a common practice in the Portland area. People remodel their homes and become certified to accept up to five residents. Each resident has his or her own bedroom. Meals are served family style, and they share the common areas of the house. Not only is it less expensive than a nursing home, but the residents benefit from the homelike atmosphere.

"My sister and I spent six weeks looking into various homes until we finally settled on one. Daddy was one of five residents, three women and two men. They ate their meals together in the dining room. The first couple of nights, there was little or no conversation. Daddy was a very social person, so it didn't take long before he had people talking. He also began saying prayers before meals.

"Daddy slowly became friends with the residents and developed their trust. His nightly ritual was to walk around to all the residents' rooms and pray with them before they went to bed.

"The most amazing thing is that Daddy only lived in that home for three months before he died, but during that short time he changed the whole atmosphere with his Christian witness. He even witnessed to them after his death, as all his worldly possessions were left to the other residents. One man was in dire need of clothes, so all Daddy's clothes were left to him. That same man loved TV but couldn't afford one of his own, so Daddy also left him his TV and recliner. Daddy had a big collection of Christian records, tapes, and old movies. One of the women loved to come to his room and borrow them, so all those were left to her.

"I have no doubt," said Pattie, "that it was God's plan for Daddy to spend his last three months of life witnessing to those people. It shows that it's never too late and you are never too old to be a light in the world."

The insurance women had tears in their eyes as they listened to Pattie's story. One of them said, "I don't know when I have ever heard a testimony like that about a Christian witness. You have changed me by your story."

Pattie said, "God doesn't make mistakes. He led me to tell you that story about Daddy. You were meant to hear his story. It's exciting to think that he is still witnessing to people, even after his death."

> *Dear Heavenly Father, this story began with Pattie's prayer that you would use her more to witness to others. Thank you for answering that simple but powerful prayer in such an amazing way. Thank you for her father who witnessed about you until the very end of his life. His witness continues to bless us even after his death. In the name of Jesus Christ we pray. Amen.*

68

Say "I Love You" Before It's Too Late

See what this godly sorrow has produced in you.
2 CORINTHIANS 7:11

I received an e-mail from a friend named Dave with the subject line: "An Opportunity Lost." He wrote:

"If you never read another thing I ever write, please, please read this. It has taken me a couple of weeks to get to where I could write this. Two weeks ago during the middle of the afternoon, my wife called from her office, and I could tell by her tone that something was wrong. She told me that my old friend, Jerry, had been found dead that morning at work.

"What was strange was how hard it hit me. I told my wife that I didn't realize how much Jerry had meant to me throughout the years. In fact, he supported me through a devastating two-year period and remained a steadfast friend, when others I thought were my friends melted away into the fog. For days now I've beat up on myself for not telling Jerry somewhere along the way how much I appreciated him and his friendship, even through difficult times. I'm heartbroken that I never actually told him. And worst of all, I don't recall sharing Christ with my friend.

"Do not write to me saying how sorry you are about my friend," wrote Dave. "I don't need that. What I do need is for you, for all of us, to make a conscious effort to tell those we care about how much they mean to us. Please don't wait. Please. It's heartbreaking. Hand out the flowers now, before you have to send them to the visitation."

Thanks, Dave, for this reminder. Your opportunity lost is our opportunity gained.

Dear Heavenly Father, maybe it's our human nature that allows us to take our friends for granted. Guide and direct us to show our love to one another when we have the opportunity. And most important, give us the boldness to witness to them about the love of your son Jesus Christ. It is in his name that we pray. Amen.

69

A Second Chance to Love My Father

For I am convinced that neither death nor life . . .
nor anything else in all creation, will be able to separate us
from the love of God that is in Christ Jesus.

ROMANS 8:38-39

"Two years ago I was given a second chance to love my father," began Josh at the funeral service for his dad, Wes. "When he was diagnosed with cancer, he was given only two months to live, but by the grace of God, that two months turned into two years.

"Before that time, I didn't know my father very well. I chose to see the man my father wasn't instead of the man he was. I focused on what I didn't have in a father instead of taking time to appreciate what I did have.

"The father I saw after the cancer diagnosis was the father who got up at 5 AM every day to spend time with God. I saw the Christian example my father left. He was a man filled with humility, a man devoted to God and family before himself. I remember the man who taught me by example that it takes effort on my part to be a Christian. He also taught me that no matter how good we are, we still need God's grace.

"When I looked at my father lying in the hospital bed in the intensive care unit, I was filled with honor and a bit overwhelmed at the standards he left behind. I know I have big shoes to fill. My father showed me how to live, and then he showed me how to die. He never gave up on life, because he knew that dying wasn't the end but rather the beginning of eternal life."

"I was fortunate to get a second chance, but you might not be as fortunate. Don't be left with a world of regrets for things left unsaid or of time wasted. It took almost losing him two years ago for me to realize fully how much I loved my father. We have only today, and we have two choices with the time we have: Either make the most of every moment and love for the time we have, or look back and have regrets for time wasted."

Wes chose Romans 8:38-39 to be read at his funeral: "For I am convinced that neither death nor life . . . nor anything else in all creation, will be able to separate us from the love of God that is in Christ Jesus." He wanted others to have that same assurance.

Josh ended his tribute to his father with this challenge: "If you died today, would you go to heaven? If you cannot answer that question with certainty, then talk to someone and pray about it. Make a choice now that can last for eternity."

> *Dear Heavenly Father, thank you that Josh received a second chance to know and love his earthly father. In that process, he received a second chance to know and love you, his Heavenly Father, in a new way. He has become a powerful witness for you with his challenge to examine our faith. Help us to make a choice now that can last for eternity. In the name of Jesus Christ we pray. Amen.*

SECTION ELEVEN

GRIEF AT THE HOLIDAYS

70

Are Christians Allowed to Be Depressed?

Jesus said, "My soul is overwhelmed with sorrow to the point of death."

MARK 14:34

Thanksgiving is the traditional beginning of the holiday season leading up to Christmas. It's also that special time of year when families congregate, so it's an especially difficult time for those who have lost loved ones. That empty place at the table hurts, even years after our loved ones have passed on.

Thanksgiving Eve will always have a special meaning to me, because my father-in-law passed away on the night before Thanksgiving. We spent Thanksgiving Day making funeral arrangements and calling friends and loved ones with the news. He lived to see eighty-six Thanksgivings, and for that, we are truly grateful, but the grief still surfaces around the holiday table. It's a bittersweet time for us—a time to celebrate and remember the life of our loved one, and at the same time, give thanks for our many blessings.

I turned on my car radio and caught part of a message by a well-known Christian writer and speaker, David Jeremiah. The topic was depression. "Mental health professionals will tell you that depression is common during the holiday season," he said. Then he asked this question: "Are Christians allowed to be depressed?"

Pastor Jeremiah said, "I have heard some preachers say from the pulpit that Christians should never be depressed, that somehow we are falling short if we are not always filled with joy, but there is no biblical basis for this idea."

When I got home, I did some research on the word "depression." My concordance does not list a single reference for the word "depression" in the Bible, but I found many references to that state of mind.

In Psalm 142:3-7 David was hiding in a cave, fleeing from Saul, who was trying to kill him. Listen to these verses: "My spirit grows faint within me.... No one cares for my life.... Listen to my cry, for I am in desperate need.... Set me free from my prison."

David, whom God called "a man after my own heart," was depressed.

In our humanness, we will experience times when our God-given emotions take over. That's not a sin. God made us, he understands our emotions, and he wants us to be honest with him. Writing out your feelings can be good therapy, just as David did in the Psalms.

Even Jesus, the Son of God, experienced times of great emotional turmoil. In John 11:33-35 Jesus responded to the death of Lazarus. When he saw Mary weeping, Scripture says, "He was deeply moved in spirit and troubled.... Jesus wept."

In Mark 14:33-34, Jesus prayed in the Garden of Gethsemane. "He began to be deeply distressed and troubled.... My soul is overwhelmed with sorrow to the point of death."

If Jesus, the Son of God, expressed such sorrow, why do we think we can survive the turmoil and tragedy of this world without those emotions? It does not mean that our faith is lacking. Trust God with your emotions during the holiday season. By all means, celebrate your many blessings, but don't feel guilty when you have tinges of melancholy. God understands you better than you understand yourself.

Dear Heavenly Father, "Happy Holidays" is not always a greeting we want to hear. Draw close to us to comfort us when we are sorrowful and help us to reach out to those around us who may be depressed during the holiday season. In the name of Jesus Christ we pray. Amen.

71

Giving Thanks, Even In Grief

But thanks be to God! He gives us the victory, through our Lord Jesus Christ.

1 CORINTHIANS 15:57

The season of Thanksgiving was started by those who lost the most—the Pilgrims. Death had taken a tremendous toll on the colony at Plymouth Rock, but they gathered and gave thanks to God for the blessings they did have.

It's difficult to give thanks in the midst of hardship and grief, isn't it?

A friend shared with me, "My dad died two months before Thanksgiving, and I was having a difficult time with his death. He was a farmer, so harvest time and giving thanks was special for him. I called my sister and said I didn't want to celebrate Thanksgiving. But her reaction was: 'We should celebrate for Dad because it was his special time of the year. He planted that crop in the spring. He would want us to celebrate the harvest.'"

Even within the same family, grief can be experienced in completely different ways. Grief is intensely personal, and there is no blueprint for how to navigate through it.

Christian counselor, Dr. Norman Wright, wrote in *The Victory: Overcoming the Trials of Life*: "As Christians, death should be a passage into heaven. So those who are left behind should rejoice, right?"

Dr. Wright answers his own question this way: "While the assurance of our loved one's eternal bliss provides comfort, it cannot replace the earthly void we experience with the loss of someone special."[1]

Dr. Wright teaches that grief is a normal human emotion. It should not be short-circuited, and there are no natural timelines for grieving. Most bereaved people need long-term support in terms of months or even years.

"People should never apologize for grieving," says Dr. Wright. "It is not normal to grieve for a few days and then be all right."[2]

As Christians, we are called to "bear one another's burdens and so fulfill the law of Christ" (Galatians 6:2) So, how can we minister to someone who is grieving during the holiday season?

Remember them with a special card or a phone call. Share some fond memories of their loved one. Let them talk. Listen patiently. Pray for them. Let them know you are praying for them. Remind them of Jesus' promise of eternal life (John 3:16). Claim the promise that they will be reunited with their loved one in heaven (John 14:2-3). And love them as Jesus loves us.

> *Dear Heavenly Father, yes, we are thankful for our blessings during the holiday season, but help us in our humanness as we remember (and grieve) those who have gone before us. Help us to claim your promise in Romans 8:39 that nothing, not even death, can separate us from your love. In the name of Jesus Christ we pray. Amen.*

---

1. Wright, Norman. *The Victory: Overcoming the Trials of Life* (Richardson: Grace Products Corporation, 2000), 57.

2. Ibid. 73.

72

Gift of Comfort at the Holidays

The angel said, "This will be a sign to you: You will find a baby wrapped in cloths and lying in a manger."

LUKE 2:12

"I've always loved Christmas," said Alvia, "especially putting up the decorations. I usually start decorating right after Thanksgiving, but this year is different. My mother passed away in March, so it will be the first Christmas without her.

"I'm sentimental about Christmas decorations, and I always loved getting them out and reminiscing. My mother gave me many of them. But this year I couldn't bring myself to get them out. I felt as though something was missing."

The week after Thanksgiving a box arrived in the mail at Alvia's house from her Uncle Ray. "He lived with my mother for a year and a half before she died," Alvia explained. "I opened the box and discovered the most wonderful gift: the fifty-year-old manger scene that Mom and Dad had when they were first married. It sat under our Christmas tree every year, so I grew up looking at it. I turned the little dial on the right hand side of the stable, and it played 'Silent Night,' still working perfectly after fifty years!

"I can remember as a child sitting on the floor examining every piece, the colorful costumes of Mary and Joseph, the animals, and the angel carrying a ribbon that says 'Peace on Earth.'

"The most special piece is Baby Jesus, not the one that originally came with the set, but one that belonged to my grandmother, so it's probably seventy-five years old. My mother always made a point to tell me how special Baby Jesus was.

"Now my own children are hearing the story of the manger scene that belonged to their grandparents and the Baby Jesus that belonged to their great-grandmother. They pick up Baby Jesus and handle him with great care, just as I did as a child.

"Now, as I walk past that manger scene every day, it's a blessing and a comfort to me. God gave me the gift of peace, and the timing of it was perfect, almost as if given permission to begin celebrating Christmas. That was the missing piece."

Dear Heavenly Father, Christmastime brings a bundle of emotions—some happy, some sad. Help us to focus on the one true gift this Christmas—Jesus Christ as the babe in the manger. Thank you for the privilege of passing on from generation to generation the wonderful story about how Jesus came to us. In his name we pray. Amen.

73

First Christmas in Heaven

"Do this in remembrance of me."
LUKE 22:19

It's Monday, December 22, as I am writing this story. This close to Christmas, I would normally be doing last-minute shopping, wrapping gifts, or sending those last Christmas cards. But this year is different. Instead of writing Christmas notes, we are writing thank you notes for funeral flowers. My mother-in-law's funeral was yesterday, December 21.

She was three days short of being eighty-eight years old, so I know we shouldn't have been so surprised at her passing. But as my daughter, Nikki, said at the funeral, "She wasn't the dying type!" She was so full of life. On the day she had her heart attack, she baked nine loaves of bread and dozens of Christmas cookies. She was planning to give them to people as Christmas gifts. Feeding people was her way of showing love.

She always invited us to her house for an elaborate Christmas dinner. In fact, she already had some of the dinner prepared when she died. Homemade noodle were drying on her countertop.

Our kids want to continue the tradition and spend Christmas Day at her house in honor of her. We're going to cook those noodles. We will prepare some of those frozen vegetables she grew in the garden and put away herself. We will have her homemade bread and jam, and those cinnamon pickles she was famous for. She had a jar full of them in the refrigerator.

We will use her immaculately pressed tablecloth and linen napkins. (Yes, she still ironed!) We will set the table with her gold-trimmed china that was a wedding gift from her husband. We will set an empty place for her at the table. I know she will enjoy watching this last Christmas celebration with her earthly family.

Just as Jesus told us to eat and drink and remember him and his sacrifice for us through Holy Communion, in that same way, we will celebrate the gifts of sacrifice and unconditional love that she had for us.

I received a condolence call from a woman who was also grieving because it was the first Christmas without her mother. She said, "I have a poem a friend sent to me titled 'My First Christmas in Heaven.' Would you like a copy of it?"

"Yes, please," I said. She mailed me a copy of it. My kids read it at their grandmother's funeral, and I would like to share it with you.

My First Christmas in Heaven

I see the countless Christmas trees
Around the world below
With tiny lights like heaven's stars
Reflecting on the snow.

I hear the many Christmas songs
That people hold so dear
But the sounds of music can't compare
With the Christmas choir up here.

I have no words to tell you
The joy their voices bring
For it is beyond description
To hear the angels sing.

I know how much you miss me
I see it in your hearts
But remember, I'm not far away
Loving memories keep us from being apart.

I sent you a special gift
From my heavenly home above
I sent you each a memory
Of my everlasting love.

After all, love is a special gift
More precious than pure gold
It always was the most important
In the stories Jesus told.

Please love and keep each other
As my Father said to do
For I can't tell you of the blessings
He has in store for each of you.

So have a glorious Christmas
And wipe away that tear
Remember, I'm spending Christmas
With Jesus Christ this year.

Author Unknown[1]

Dear Lord, as we celebrate your birth at this holy time of the year, it is difficult to balance the joy we are expected to feel with the reality of the empty chair at the holiday table. Bless us with good memories of our loved ones and comfort us when we experience feelings of melancholy. It is in your name that we pray. Amen

---

[1] Several sources attribute this poem to a thirteen-year-old boy named Ben who died in 1997 after a lengthy battle with a brain tumor.

74

Will Your Passing Leave a Hole in the World?

For we are his workmanship, created in Christ Jesus for good works, which God prepared beforehand that we should walk in them.

EPHESIANS 2:10

It's difficult to celebrate the coming of a new year without thinking about those who were with us last New Year's Eve, those who have gone on to their heavenly homes. I am reminded of a sermon given after the death of a dedicated pastor in our community. The line repeated again and again in that sermon was this one: "A person who matters will leave a hole in the world. He will be missed."

That is also the theme in the classic movie, *It's a Wonderful Life*. The Christmas holiday would not be complete for many of us without watching that movie at least once. George Bailey despairs that his life has not been worth living, that he failed to accomplish anything worthwhile. Facing personal and financial problems, he attempts to end it all.

Clarence, his bumbling guardian angel, saves George and then gives him a wonderful gift: a look at how the world would have been different if he had not lived.

The best line in the movie is this one from Clarence to George Bailey: "Strange, isn't it? Each man's life touches so many other lives, and when he isn't around he leaves an awful hole to fill, doesn't he?"

A friend sent me a quote by e-mail that I keep on my desk. It says, "God sent each person into the world with a special message to deliver, a special song to sing, and a special act of love to bestow. No one else can speak my message or sing my song or offer my love . . . these are entrusted to me."

Isn't that exciting? God created each one of us uniquely to fill a specific role in the world. No one else can fill it.

New Year's Eve is a good time to take stock of yourself and ask some hard questions: How would the world be different if I had never lived? Will I leave a hole in the world when I am gone?

It's sad that many times we don't recognize the holes people leave in the world until we hear their eulogies. Suddenly we see a new aspect of that person that we did not know about or did not appreciate when he or she lived. Is that simply human nature? Do we not appreciate those people around us until they are gone? Do we wait until it's too late to say, "I love you," or "Let me tell you how you changed my life"?

Dear Heavenly Father, will my passing leave a hole in the world? Help me to know that I was created to fill a specific role in the world that no one else can fill. Let me live my life for your glory. In the name of Jesus Christ, we pray. Amen.

75

If This New Year's Eve Were Your Last....

He has made everything beautiful in its time.
He has set eternity in the hearts of men.

ECCLESIASTES 3:11

As you ring in the New Year, I want you to think about something: How would your life change if you knew this would be your last New Year's Eve?

Rev. Charles Williams of Indianapolis wrote a farewell article for *The Indianapolis Star* in 2002 titled, "Treating This Holiday As If It Were Your Last." Williams wrote:

> Though I am in the final stages of cancer and the disease has spread, I remain confident in a doctor who has never lost a patient: God.
>
> When we think about life, we sometimes function as though living is guaranteed and death is only a possibility. No matter how we try to escape discussion of our mortality, there is an inevitable end to our physical existence. Death is the common denominator of the rich and poor, black and white, male and female, young and old. None of us knows the day or the hour of our transition, so wouldn't that make rational people want to

live each day—and especially each holiday—as though it were their last?

As for me, I plan to shout an extra "Hallelujah!" and "Thank you, Jesus!" in church this Sunday. I plan to say a prayer that will shake the foundation of heaven, thanking the Lord for all the blessings I've received throughout my lifetime.[1]

How about you? If you knew without a doubt that you would not live to see next New Year's Eve, what would you do differently in the coming months?

Would you spend more quality time with your family and friends? Would you say "I love you" more often? Would you forgive a long-time grudge? Would you give away your money and possessions to the needy?

The Book of Ecclesiastes is a record of Solomon's desperate search for meaning at the end of his life. His diatribe is profoundly negative as he concludes that much of what we value on earth is meaningless. Solomon convinces us of the vanity of the world and that it cannot make us happy. No created good can satisfy the soul, he asserts.

But then we read these words of Solomon in Ecclesiastes. 3:11, "He has made everything beautiful in its time. He has also set eternity in the hearts of men."

Solomon concludes that meaning is found in God alone.

What words will you utter at the end of your life? Will you put your trust and hope in eternal life with your Lord and Savior Jesus Christ?

> *Dear Heavenly Father, help us to recognize that most of what we value on earth is meaningless. Thank you that you have, indeed, set eternity in the hearts of men and that meaning can be found in you alone. In the name of Jesus Christ we pray. Amen.*

---

1. Williams, Charles, Rev. *The Indianapolis Star*, "Treating This Holiday As If It Were Your Last." Dec. 26, 2006, B7.

SECTION TWELVE

PRECIOUS MEMORIES

76

Cleaning Out the House

The Lord remembers us and will bless us.
PSALM 115:12

"My parents were remarkable people," said Kay.

Kay was grieving the loss of her parents who passed away within nine months of each other. Her mother died in March, and her dad died the following November.

"Mother and Dad remained active in their church and in their small community of Wingate, Indiana, until they died," Kay continued. "In fact, Dad was the oldest town board president in the state when he died at ninety-four, and Mother was still writing feature columns as a correspondent for the *Journal & Review* in Crawfordsville, Indiana, when she passed away at ninety-two."

They lived in the same house for sixty years, so it was a difficult task when Kay had to clean it out. In the back of a closet, she discovered a little square-shaped suitcase with a plastic handle. Kay said, "It brought back a lot of memories because I took that little suitcase to many slumber parties in my youth. When I opened it, there was only one thing in it: an index card in Mother's handwriting that said, 'I love you.'

"That was quite remarkable to me, because my parents were not real demonstrative in their expressions of love, something that was common of many people in their generation. Don't get me wrong, I knew without a doubt I was loved, but there were not a lot of hugs or 'I love you's.' Mother knew I would find that note in that suitcase. It was a wonderful gift."

Kay explained that the old house had been on the market nearly two years, but it still hadn't sold. "We were in the process of listing it with a new real estate agent. It was during a brutal, midsummer heat wave when my husband and I spent three grueling days there mowing the grass, trimming the bushes, and cleaning the house.

"My final task before the new agent arrived was to scrub the kitchen floor. I thought about Mother as I was on my knees scrubbing that floor as I had done since I was ten years old. I thought, *I hope this is the last time I have to clean this old floor!* Mother was an immaculate housekeeper, so I know she would have appreciated my efforts to make it look better.

"After the real estate agent left, friends came by to take us to dinner. 'Oh, your parents had a Purdue mailbox!' they exclaimed.

"Yes, they were great Purdue fans. You can have it if you want it."

"Do you think there's any mail in it?"

"Oh, no," answered Kay. "There hasn't been any mail here for two years."

But when Kay's friend opened the mailbox, she found a copy of a newspaper—the one her mother used to write for!

"It was such a shock to see that paper in there," said Kay, "but I didn't have time to look at it, so I threw the paper in the car to read at home later. A few days later, I picked it up again. I always enjoyed reading about the local community activities. I felt such a strong connection to my mother as I held that paper in my hands. She wrote for them for forty-five years.

"But the part that caught my attention was the date of the paper. It had been placed in that mailbox two weeks earlier on June 29, a very special date—my birthday! You had to know my mother to understand how significant that was. Birthdays in my family were always a big thing. Mother made sure we all had our special celebration. I knew this was Mother's way of remembering my birthday and God's way of comforting me."

Dear Heavenly Father, thank you for the special gifts of remembrance you give us when we are grieving. Open our eyes to these little incidents of comfort that can only come from you. In the name of Jesus Christ we pray. Amen.

77

In Remembrance of a Soldier

No man knows when his hour will come.

ECCLESIASTES 9:12

"Dear Mom and Dad, It looks like we may go overseas for duty in two or three months. I don't think we will ever go in the fighting zone. The old saying is 'a good soldier never dies' so don't think too much about it. I'm one of the best! Your Soldier, Eugene"

That letter postmarked July 16, 1944, was from my husband's Uncle Gene, a twenty-eight-year-old infantryman in the Army in World War II. Unfolding that yellowed letter was like taking a sixty-year step back in a time machine.

Our family was going through a difficult but necessary task when we found that letter. My mother-in-law died, so we were going through all her worldly goods, preparing to sell her house. What should be saved? What should be discarded? Even the smallest items evoked memories we didn't want to let go of, and the emotions attached to certain items were heartrending.

In one drawer, we found visitors' registers from funerals of my husband's grandparents. We found Uncle Gene's letter stuck in one of those books. My mother-in-law, Gene's sister, was his last surviving sibling, so she inherited all the papers relating to his military service.

In a large manila envelope, I found a letter from the U.S. Army dated December 7, 1944: "It is with profound regret that I confirm the recent telegram informing you of the death of your son . . . ." One month later a proclamation signed by Franklin D. Roosevelt awarded Gene the Purple Heart "for wounds received in action resulting in death."

Also included in his papers was a picture of a U.S. Military Cemetery where Gene was buried in Limey, France, with row upon row of white crosses stretching as far as the eye could see. A letter from the War Department states: "Here rest the remains of those heroic dead who fell together in the service of our country. It is my sincere hope that you may gain some solace from this view of the surroundings in which your loved one rests."

As I looked at that picture of those white crosses, a profound sadness came over me. I thought: *Each of those young soldiers thought he would be returning home to a normal life, but instead, gave the ultimate sacrifice for his country. That old saying, "good soldiers never die," is not true. Rain falls on the just and on the unjust.*

The writer in Ecclesiastes 9:12 says: "No man knows when his hour will come . . . men are trapped by evil times that fall unexpectedly upon them."

If your life were to end tomorrow, would you be ready? None of us can escape physical death, but we can choose to live in eternal life when we have Jesus Christ as our Lord and Savior.

Dear Heavenly Father, help us remember the supreme sacrifice of those soldiers who gave their lives for our country. Remind us also of your son Jesus Christ, who gave the supreme sacrifice so that we can live in eternal life with you. In his name we pray. Amen.

78

He Raced into the Arms of Jesus

*I have fought the good fight, I have finished the race,
I have kept the faith.*

2 TIMOTHY 4:7

If you happened to see a funeral procession winding through Frankfort, Indiana, on August 15, 2007, you might have noticed something unusual: in front of the hearse was a black and white checkered pace car in honor of Bob Lemen, Jr., age fifty-nine, who died at Anderson Speedway on Saturday, August 11. No, he didn't die in a racing accident. He died of a heart attack just after crossing the finish line in the forty-lap Super Truck race.

Bob's love of racing began at an early age. Pictures at the funeral home showed him at age four standing next to his midget racer. His dad, Bob Lemen, Sr., raced stock cars at the Anderson Speedway track many times, so Bob, Jr. grew up in a family that loved racing.

At age forty-seven Bob began a new love: racing Super Trucks. He was known around Indiana for his Super Truck #47. Bob's dad and mom were familiar faces in the stands during their son's races as they followed his career. In fact, they were present the night Bob died.

After Bob's death, the president of Anderson Speedway said, "Bob was a true champion in every sense of the word, both on and off the track. He died doing what he loved best. Bob really wanted to win a championship, which means you end up with more points than anyone else does at the end of the season. Bob's season ended Saturday as the point leader, which means to me that he left this world as the champion of Anderson Speedway."

Bob was a champion both on and off the racetrack. He was a dedicated member of his church in Indianapolis. His pastor said, "Bob was the audio tech at our church. Every Sunday morning he worked on the soundboard. His love of racing kept him at the track until 1 or 2 AM on Saturday nights, but every Sunday morning at 8:45, he was there to perform his duties.

"He wasn't a Sunday morning Christian," continued the pastor. "He was a substitute Sunday school teacher in an adult class and a faithful member of our Wednesday night Bible study. He was always quick to volunteer for church workdays with his chain saw or whatever was needed. I remember Bob as a quiet, dependable man with a strong faith."

A friend of mine at the funeral looked around at all of Bob's racing trophies on display. She whispered, "I think I could preach this sermon. I'll bet the pastor will talk about finishing the race."

She was referring to the apostle Paul's words from a Roman prison. Paul knew the end of his life was near when he wrote to his trusted friend Timothy: "The time has come for my departure. I have fought the good fight, I have finished the race, I have kept the faith. Now there is in store for me the crown of righteousness, which the Lord, the righteous judge, will award to me on that day." (2 Timothy 4:7-8)

As predicted, the pastor began the eulogy with those verses, and he concluded with these words: "I am sure Bob was proud of every trophy he won over the years, but I hope you can picture him now, not standing at the finish line of some race track, but standing within heaven's gates. He isn't holding a trophy as much as a crown. It is Jesus Christ himself congratulating him and saying: 'Well done, good and faithful servant!'"

Yes, I think Bob raced right into the arms of Jesus.

Dear Heavenly Father, thank you for Bob's life both on and off the racetrack. Bob died doing what he loved best in the middle of a winning season. But his life exemplified what Paul said to Timothy, "Be prepared in season and out of season." (2 Tim. 4:2) We can all follow his example as we run with perseverance the race marked out for us. In the name of Jesus Christ we pray. Amen.

79

A Life That Matters

For whoever finds Me finds life.

PROVERBS 8:35

On Sunday, December 7, 2003, Brian said to his pastor, "Hey, why don't you go to the archives and pull out that sermon you gave several years ago called 'A Life That Matters.' I lost my tape of it."

"I was just thinking about that sermon," said Pastor Wayne. "I'll preach it next Sunday."

No one could have known how prophetic Brian's request was. The next morning, December 8, at 7:45 AM, Brian died in an automobile accident. He was only forty-one years old.

Brian was a dedicated Christian man who had a long history of volunteer work with youth at his church. For three years before he died, he worked with high school kids in Youth for Christ, an organization that develops students' relationships with Jesus and then steers them to a church home. Brian helped lead their weekly meetings and formed deep friendships with many of the kids.

Brian lived a life that mattered to hundreds, maybe thousands, of people. Pastor Wayne said, "Brian had an urgency to reach young people. He belonged to a small group of adults who met at the church every week to pray and study. The day before he died, Brian asked them to pray for one young girl in particular. He said, 'Something has to be done because we don't know how much time she has.' Brian didn't know that it was his time that was short."

The mother of one of the teens he shepherded said, "Brian had a special burden for teens who needed a dad. He fathered the fatherless. He loved the unlovable and made a difference in their lives. Brian had the gift of teaching people about God's unconditional love through personal relationships. We can all love the easy ones," she continued, "but he loved the kids other people gave up on. He took kids into his home and made every one of them feel special. For every story you hear about Brian and his impact on kids, probably ten or twenty others could tell the same story. Brian made each of them feel that their life was a life that mattered."

Brian's funeral was on December 12, with a tremendous outpouring of love from the community. A thousand people went through the line to pay their condolences, some waiting more than two hours. Four hundred people filled the church auditorium for his service, and $2,000 was donated to youth ministry.

Brian would have been embarrassed at all the accolades he received when he died, because he always wanted God to get the credit. In fact, two weeks before Brian died he told a friend, "God is blessing me abundantly. Everything I touch turns to gold." He knew without a doubt that his blessings came from God.

Pastor Wayne went ahead with his plans to give that sermon again, "A Life That Matters," on December 14, two days after Brian's funeral and exactly one week after Brian requested it. One of the main points of the sermon was this: "A life that matters will be missed. It will leave a hole that will be hard to fill."

The impact of that message was magnified a thousandfold by Brian's passing. Brian left a big hole in the world, but now we are witnessing the fruit of his life, with many new people attending church and others recommitting their lives to Christ. In our humanness, we grieve his passing. But we also rejoice with the angels in heaven that we were given the gift of his life on this earth and that he has eternal life with Jesus Christ.

Dear Heavenly Father, thank you for the gift of Brian's life. Instill in us Brian's sense of urgency to share the Gospel. Time is short! How will people hear unless we tell them? And how will people know God's love unless we show them? Give us the courage to ask: Is my life a life that matters? In the name of Jesus Christ we pray. Amen.

80

You Won't Be Crippled in Heaven

Your God will come . . . then will the lame leap like a deer.

ISAIAH 35:4, 6

A man named John called me with a story about his seventy-year-old sister, Ruthie, who died suddenly. He wanted to tell me about her life.

"Ruthie was truly a special person. She was a strong Christian and a very giving person. Maybe she developed into such a special person because of the difficult life she lived. Ruthie was born in 1933, a perfectly healthy little girl. She was eighteen months old when she contracted polio. Her temperature was 105 degrees for a week, which caused permanent damage to the left side of her brain. For the rest of her life Ruthie suffered from seizures and stroke-like symptoms on the right side of her body. She couldn't use her right hand, and she walked with a limp.

"When she started school, the kids were mean to her and made fun of her. She came home in tears many days, but my father always comforted her with the same story: 'One day Jesus will come down out of the sky and take you up to heaven. Then you will be perfect. You won't be crippled in heaven.'

"Many times I remember Ruthie begging: 'Daddy, tell me again the story about when I get to heaven.' He told the story the same way every time, always ending with, 'You won't be crippled in heaven.'

"When the situation at school became unbearable for her, my dad took her out of school and said: 'We'll educate her at home.'

"I admired my sister greatly. I wrote a song in her honor called 'You Won't Be Crippled in Heaven.' That song was played at her funeral, and there wasn't a dry eye in the house."

Jesus promises in John 14:2-3, "I am going there [to heaven] to prepare a place for you. . . . I will come back and take you to be with me." In Isaiah 35:4 and 6, the prophet Isaiah speaks about the joys of the redeemed, including perfect health. "Your God will come . . . then will the lame leap like a deer."

Dear Lord, thank you for Ruthie's life and for John's tribute to his sister. What wonderful promises you make to us! No matter what our physical states are here on earth, we are made perfect in heaven. Thank you for that promise. In the name of Jesus Christ we pray. Amen.

SECTION THIRTEEN

WHY, GOD?

81

When We Do Not Understand

Jesus wept. Then the Jews said, "See how he loved him!"
JOHN 11:35-36

September 14, 2001, was designated as a National Day of Mourning after the 9/11 terrorist attacks in New York City, Pennsylvania, and Washington D.C. Coincidentally, my church family also experienced a tragedy that week after the death of triplets born prematurely to our Pastor Lore. The funeral for those babies was also on September 14, and I couldn't help comparing the grief we shared that day to the grief of our nation.

The title of the message at the funeral was, "When We Do Not Understand." In the opening prayer Pastor John said, "Eternal and loving God, we come with mournful hearts seeking the peace, which only you can give. We confess that life often confuses us, leaving us groping for some meaning amid the mysteries we do not understand. Enable us, Lord, to find your healing light in our time of darkness, your comfort for the hurt that runs deep within, and your strength to see us all through what we face now and whatever comes in the future. Amen."

That beautiful prayer spoken at the funeral for three innocent babies could have been spoken at our National Day of Mourning when thousands of innocent people were remembered.

I think about the intense sorrow in Pastor Lore's family and in our church family over the loss of those babies. And then I try to multiply in my mind that same sorrow thousands of times for the lives lost in this national tragedy. It's more than my mind can comprehend. Man doesn't have words to describe the depths of that kind of sorrow.

Does God shed as many tears for the loss of one as for the loss of thousands?

Jesus' humanity and the depth of his sorrow over the death of one person were expressed perfectly in the shortest verse in the Bible, John 11:35, "Jesus wept." Jesus was heartbroken at the death of his friend, Lazarus. When the Jews saw his tears, they said, "See how he loved him!" His tears, just like our tears, were the perfect expression of sorrow.

Jesus also wept at their unbelief. He knew that Lazarus would be raised from the dead, but still he wept with compassion for the grief of his friends and relatives.

God is not a stranger to sorrow. He experienced the sorrow of his innocent son dying a cruel death on a cross, bearing the sins of the world. God must experience another kind of sorrow, too, the kind he must feel when we fall away from him both personally and as a country. His heart breaks with sorrow for our fallen world and for the people who will not know him when they die.

> *Dear God, no, we do not understand the loss of three innocent babies or the loss of thousands in our national tragedy, but we know that you weep with us when we suffer. You are not only a God of compassion, you are a God of resurrection and eternal life. Just as these babies will live eternally with you in heaven, just as Lazarus was raised from the dead, and just as Jesus was resurrected from the grave, so can we as a nation be resurrected from the ashes. Rebuild our fallen world as you bring us back to your son, Jesus Christ. It is in his name that we pray. Amen.*

82

No One Is Exempt

*In this world you will have tribulation; but be of good cheer,
I have overcome the world.*

JOHN 16:33

My Wednesday morning prayer group gathered around a friend named Sharon, who was just diagnosed with cancer. About ten of us circled her chair and laid hands on her in prayer. One of the women prayed, "No one is exempt from struggles in life, but we have the promise that you always walk with us through the valleys."

That prayer brought to mind a sermon where the pastor used that same phrase: "No one is exempt."

Those words had special meaning to our congregation because our Pastor Lore gave that sermon four months after she lost triplets born prematurely. People struggled to understand the loss of those babies. One of the statements I heard was, "She's a minister. She has given her life to God. It's not fair! Why would something like that happen to her?"

Pastor Lore's response to that in her sermon was, "No one is exempt."

She's right, of course. Even Jesus Christ, the Son of God, was not exempt from pain, suffering, and physical death.

Dear Lord Jesus, You did not promise to keep us from trials, but to be with us through the trials. You didn't promise ease, but you did promise strength for the journey. Thank you for that. It is in your name we pray. Amen.

83

Trust in the Lord with All Your Heart

Trust in the Lord with all your heart and lean not on your own understanding.

PROVERBS 3:5

One of our dear friends, only sixty years old, was near death in an Indianapolis hospital. Yes, we knew she would be with our Lord and Savior, but it was still difficult to let her go. It's easy to ask that age-old question: "Why, Lord? She's too young to die. She is needed here!"

I prayed for God to speak to me about this. In response, the Lord showed me a story I started to write nearly four months earlier.

I met a woman named Barbara in Seattle, Washington. She, too, was struggling with the death of her forty-two-year-old brother, Mark. He was in intensive care dying of cancer at a time that should have been the prime of his life.

"The last time I was with him," she said, "I felt compelled to read him a Bible verse, Proverbs 3:5-6: 'Trust in the Lord with all your heart and lean not on your own understanding. In all your ways acknowledge him, and he will make your paths straight.'

"In fact, the feeling I had about that verse was so strong that I wrote it on a little card and left it with him. He was still hanging on when I left the hospital for the three-hour drive home.

"A few days later, I was getting ready for work. It must have been around 6 or 7 AM. Suddenly I felt an overwhelming urge to go to the side of my bed and get down on my knees. I knelt and prayed: 'God, I don't know what this means. All I know is that you are calling me to pray right now.'

"God kept reminding me of that verse from Proverbs: 'Trust in the Lord with all your heart and lean not on your own understanding.'

"I finished getting ready for work. On the drive there, I kept repeating Proverbs 3:5-6, 'Trust in the Lord with all your heart . . .' A few minutes after I arrived, I got a phone call from my sister saying Mark had just died."

I read this story and wondered how God could be using it to speak to me. After all, Mark still died much too young.

In answer, God led me to a book I had not looked at in a long time called *Is That You, Lord?* by Roberta Rogers. In a section called "But I Don't Understand!" she wrote:

> God's ways are not our ways and his thoughts are not our thoughts. As vast as the universe towering above our heads, that far beyond our comprehension is the mind of God (Isaiah. 55:9). . . . "Why, God?" is seldom a good question, and it will seldom get us an answer. . . . Most of our questions will remain unanswered until we get to heaven. . . . Life here, as pleasant as it can be with friends and family and laughter and love, is nothing compared to life with our Heavenly Father. . . . It's okay to ask God unanswerable things. And it is okay for him not to tell you now, or ever. He is still God. He is both wise and good. He knows when we frail humans simply cannot understand something in any way he can communicate to us now. Our faith must make up the difference.[1]

In other words, trust in the Lord with all your heart and lean not on your own understanding.

Dear Heavenly Father, when your son Jesus died on the cross, the disciples did not understand. They could not comprehend your eternal plan. It is the same with us today. Teach us that faith is always beyond human reasoning or it would not be faith. Thank you for the promise that we will live in eternity with you. In the name of Jesus Christ we pray. Amen.

---

1. Rogers, Roberta. *Is That You, Lord?* (Grand Rapids: Chosen Books, 2000), 158-161.

84

Are You Stuck in Grief?

The disciples were together, with the doors locked for fear of the Jews.

JOHN 20:19

What do you do on Saturday of Easter weekend? That's a good question for Christians.

Jesus was crucified on Friday. The resurrection occurred on Sunday. What did the disciples do on Saturday? We don't know for certain, but it's a pretty good guess that they were together in the Upper Room where they had shared The Last Supper with Jesus the night before his arrest. Now they were hunted men. As followers of Jesus, they could be the next to die.

They were probably filled with questions: Why did this happen? What purpose does his death serve? Why did he have to suffer? What are we supposed to do now?

Have you ever been stuck on Saturday, filled with doubt and despair? Perhaps you can identify with the disciples' questions. Maybe a loved one died, and you don't understand why. Maybe a friend has been diagnosed with terminal cancer or your child is suffering from an incurable disease.

Whatever the reason, you may be stuck on Saturday, asking the same questions as the disciples: Why did this happen? What purpose does this serve? Why do people have to suffer? What am I supposed to do now?

One of my favorite Christian authors is Catherine Marshall. Her husband, Peter Marshall, was a much-loved minister in Washington, D.C., when he died of a heart attack at the age of forty-four. Catherine was left with their young son to rear on her own. In her devotional book, *Moments That Matter*[1], she wrote:

> Looking back, I can see that the most exciting events of my life have all risen out of trouble: my three-year illness that forced me into a spiritual exploration that revolutionized my personal Christian living; then the deep valley of Peter's death and the door that eventually opened into a writing career for me. In fact, the deeper the difficulty, the more dramatic the creativity God has brought from it.

Catherine Marshall related her experience to the Easter season with these words:

> On Good Friday long ago evil surged to its climax on a hill shaped like a skull. But the empty tomb of Easter morning says to you and me, "Of course you'll encounter trouble. But behold a God of power who can take any evil and turn it into a door of hope."

Is your life filled with Saturdays—days of fear, loneliness, and despair? Or have you experienced the joy of Easter morning, when the stone was rolled away?

> *Dear Heavenly Father, we thank you for your son Jesus Christ, who died on the cross so that our sins could be forgiven. Help us to get past Saturday to the joy of the resurrection on Sunday morning. In the name of Jesus Christ we pray. Amen.*

---

1. Marshall, Catherine. *Moments that Matter: Inspiration for Each Day of the Year.* Nashville. Countryman, a Division of Thomas Nelson, Inc., 2001, 101.

85

Let Go of Your Anger

Give ear to my words, O LORD, *consider my sighing.*
Listen to my cry for help, my King and my God.

PSALM 5:1-2

After the Sunday morning church service, some friends of mine went to a restaurant for lunch. Their waiter, Jason, had taken their orders. One of the group offered a blessing for the food and concluded with these words: "And we ask a special blessing on Jason, our waiter."

They enjoyed good fellowship around the table during dinner. Jason overheard bits and pieces of the conversation as he waited on their table, so he knew they were a church group. "Is one of you a pastor?" he asked.

"Yes. I am," answered one of the men.

Jason stood next to the pastor and said, "I haven't been to church in nine years."

Sensing an opportunity to witness to Jason, he asked, "What happened nine years ago that made you leave the church?"

"My dad died when I was eleven years old."

"Are you angry with God about that?"

After a short hesitation, Jason said, "Yes, I am. I had a hard life after he died. I don't understand why God let that happen to my family."

"Read the Psalms," recommended the pastor. "David was angry with God many times. It's not wrong to be angry with God. He wants to know your true feelings. He wants you to be honest with him. Sometimes after you vent your anger, then you can turn back to God."

Sitting next to the preacher was a woman named Ann, who was listening to the conversation. She reached out to Jason and said, "I know how you feel. My husband was killed in a farming accident nine years ago. I was totally devastated and didn't know how I could go on without him. I had a lot of fear about the future, and some anger too. But I decided I had two choices. Either I could turn my back on God, or I could turn toward him and ask for his help. I chose to turn to God, and I have never regretted it."

Jason asked for the pastor's name and address and said he would be in touch with him. That simple prayer, "God bless the waiter," turned into an opportunity to witness to a young man who had never dealt with his anger and grief.

Dear Heavenly Father, thank you that Jason was able to open up to a complete stranger about his anger at you. And thank you for the people you provided to witness to him at that moment. In the name of Jesus Christ we pray. Amen.

86

Run the Race Set before You

Let us run with perseverance the race marked out for us.

HEBREWS 12:1

I love that Bible verse about running the race set before you, often quoted at funerals. Those words took on a completely new meaning after I finished reading twenty-one pages of eulogies and remembrances for a remarkable young medical missionary named Brianna.

A friend, whose daughter roomed with Bri for two years at college, referred me to a Web site about Brianna's life and death. Brianna, only twenty-five years old, was killed in a traffic accident in Nigeria while on the mission field as a nurse/mid-wife.

Dan Wogelmuth, President of Youth for Christ World Outreach, wrote a tribute to Bri, describing her as one who "escorted infant Africans out of their mothers' wombs. She did so with compassion and grace, ministering to hurting, frightened, and worried mothers. She loved her job, both the medical and the spiritual." [1]

In his eulogy for Bri he said, "Her short life was like the 100-meter dash, completed in a matter of seconds, compared to the 800- and 1500-meter races, which consume minutes. Each racer locks into their particular distance and runs with passion and determination over the prescribed course. What you don't find are sprinters complaining that their race simply wasn't long enough, or distance runners whining about the grueling length of their race. Whatever the course, they ran with all they had. Our race is the distance the Father has selected for us to run.

"Brianna's race is over. Yes, it seemed a good bit like a 100-meter dash. While it's easy to want for more, this was the full length of her race. She did it well. In the short time that defined her, she lived her life to the full."

What a wonderful way to look at a life that we think was cut short: Our race is the distance the Father has selected for us to run. Jesus died at thirty-three, but in those thirty-three years, he completely fulfilled God's purpose for him on this earth.

> *Dear Heavenly Father, although sometimes it is difficult to accept, help us remember that our race is the distance you have selected for us to run. Help us to run with passion and endurance the race that is set before us, to your honor and glory. In the name of Jesus Christ we pray. Amen.*

---

1. Wogelmuth, Dan, entry on website: http//www.bethanylutheran.org/brimemories.html, Dec. 16, 2005, p. 1.

87

Looking for Jesus

*But Mary [Magdalene] stood outside by the tomb weeping . . .
She turned around and saw Jesus standing there,
and did not know that it was Jesus.*

JOHN 20:11, 14

In the previous story, I wrote about Brianna, a young medical missionary who served as a midwife in Nigeria at a city hospital. She died in a traffic accident. Her monthly prayer letter arrived in mailboxes in the U.S. a week after she died. She wrote:

> Every day, my team and I minister to pregnant women through prenatal care, labor, delivery and postnatal care. We have learned the importance of "being with a woman" as she faces challenges at each of these stages.
> The birth of a child is always a special moment. As the mother catches a glimpse of her new child, there is a new understanding of the greatness of God's love and the miracle of this new created life. A sudden understanding of the depth, and height, the width and length of the love and compassion of Christ suddenly comes upon me as this new mother beholds the sight of her precious child. The joy in her eyes takes away any of the pain and suffering she has just come through. I am able to join in and celebrate her triumph with her.

Unfortunately, not every delivery comes with a happy ending. We have seen many tragedies along the way. Even though we are in a hospital, we still face the common circumstances of a developing country, including a lack of resources, lack of education, and poverty. Joy comes slowly in these circumstances and many times, I find it difficult to see how God is working. But I trust that he is there, and as I come alongside these grieving women, somehow I learn how to show them Jesus' compassion as he reveals himself to me.

Bri went on to talk about two patients she ministered to.

A woman named Patience came into the hospital bleeding both physically and emotionally. She carried her baby for nine months, but he died in the womb. She came to deliver him, with no hope of finally meeting her child face to face or of hearing his first cry. As she walked into the delivery room, tears streaming down her face, I helped her onto the bed and held her hand as she pushed out her lifeless child. As I wiped the tears from her eyes, my own spilled down my cheeks, and I wept with her. That next week was spent in a mixture of tears and laughter as we both processed through the loss of her child and the hope of what God had for her in the future.

Another patient, Mary, came into the hospital and was placed in the isolation ward with a dangerous infection from obstructed labor. When she delivered the lifeless baby, we were shocked at the decay. As I held her hand, my heart broke, and I stood in frantic wonder, looking to find Jesus in that room. Just as Mary Magdalene looked for Jesus in the empty tomb and then did not recognize him in the garden, we often come across circumstances where we don't recognize him either, but we trust that he is there.

As her friends and family around the world struggled with the "why" questions of Bri's death, a friend named Nicole wrote, "I am struck now that my friend wrote these words a week before she was to leave this earth, words that would minister to me in my grief over her passing."

Another friend added, "Perhaps Brianna was preparing us in her last prayer letter for our own sense of 'frantic wonder.' Sometimes we don't recognize Jesus in the empty tomb, and yet he is there."

Dear Jesus, yes, there are times when we feel a sense of "frantic wonder," as we look for you in the midst of human suffering. But we know you are there, watching over us, weeping with us, and comforting us. It is in your name we pray. Amen.

88

The Mystery of It All

"Can you fathom the mysteries of God?"

JOB 11:7

"God, why didn't you let us be with him when he died? We didn't get a chance to say goodbye to him!"

Those words came from the grandchildren of a man who passed away unexpectedly. He died alone, despite the fact that the entire family was nearby. In fact, one of the granddaughters visited him two hours earlier. He had been ill, but there was no indication that he wouldn't make it through the night. They felt cheated.

Health professionals said it's not unusual for people to die alone, almost as if they choose to die that way to spare the family, but that was little consolation. They prayed for God to give them some peace about it.

Two weeks later a guest pastor at their church told this story: "Ten years ago my mother called me from New York City crying and said, 'I just called to say it's all right. I'm on my way home.'"

The pastor said, "I understood the code language and the 'home' she was referring to, but I refused to believe it because she wasn't even ill at the time. But she kept repeating the same message: 'I'm on my way home, but it's going to be all right.'"

A few days later, he got a phone call that his mother was admitted to the hospital. It was nothing life threatening, he was assured, but the next morning he caught an early flight to New York. "I wanted to surprise her," he said.

But he was the one surprised. When he arrived at the hospital, he learned she had died alone while he was en route.

"Why, God?" he pleaded. "You knew I wanted to be there with my mother when she died!

"It's a mystery," continued the pastor. "We do not like mystery. We want to have answers to all our questions, but sometimes we have to trust God at that place of mystery."

In a strange sort of way, his sermon was an answer for those grieving grandchildren. Some things in this earthly life will always be mysteries because our human minds can't comprehend the things of God.

The pastor quoted Paul from 1 Corinthians 13:11-12, "Now we see but a poor reflection in a mirror; then we shall see face to face. Now I know in part; then I shall know fully."

Paul spoke of our imperfect knowledge during this age, comparing it to a mirror of poor quality, which gives only a dim reflection. But the good news is that when we see God face to face, our knowledge will be full and complete.

As I took a break from writing, God led me to one of my devotional books, *God Calling*, by A. J. Russell, which often speaks to me in powerful ways. I wasn't disappointed as I turned to the lesson for that day. It was titled, "Mysteries." This is what it said:

> Do not try to find answers to the mysteries of the world. Learn to know me more and more, and in that knowledge you will have all the answers you need here, and when you see me face to face, in that purely spiritual world, you will find no need to ask.[1]

Dear God, we don't understand your ways here on earth, but we do understand that when we see you face to face, all our questions will be answered. In the name of Jesus Christ we pray. Amen.

---

1. Russell, A. J. *God Calling*. (Uhrichsville: Barbour and Company, Inc., 1989), 220.

SECTION FOURTEEN

GROWTH THROUGH GRIEF

89

From Wailing to Singing

With singing lips my mouth will praise you.
PSALM 63:5

For sixteen years, missionaries, Andy and Audrey Minch, worked and lived with the people of Amanab, Sandaun Province, in New Guinea. They translated the New Testament into the Amanab language. One of their co-translators, Charles Nuwei, dedicated his life to traveling to remote villages to distribute copies of the New Testament.

A newsletter from Andy and Audrey in the spring of 2006 brought some tragic news. They wrote:

> On March 20 we learned of the death of our good friend and colleague, Charles Nuwei, in his early 30s, leaving a wife and three small children. Charles was struck and killed by lightning while attending a Bible school in another province.
>
> In addition to translating and distributing copies of the Amanab New Testament, Charles was a successful Christian businessman. As a community leader, he initiated a rice project to enable the village to pay for their children's school fees. He was a respected church leader and evangelist involved with youth, sports, and music. His Christianity was integrated into every aspect of community life.

On March 29, Andy and Audrey received word from a colleague that between two and three hundred people waited at the grassy airstrip when the plane took Charles' body back to Amanab for burial. Their colleague described the scene that met the plane:

> Instead of the usual wailing and emotional scenes that are typical to the area at the time of a death, the Amanab people stood there singing! The village women continued to sing even as the afternoon rain turned into a downpour. In tribute to Charles, his soccer teammates in full uniform bore his plywood coffin off the plane. There was an unmistakable atmosphere of God's presence. We were all very moved by the sacredness of the occasion.

We often noted while at Amanab that death reveals people's deepest beliefs. There is no pretending. Although Charles' death brought much sorrow, it also demonstrated to the unbelieving Amanab community the hope that Christians have in Christ and in eternal life. This transformation was clearly proclaimed through the testimony of their singing.

Dear Heavenly Father, Thank you for the powerful witness that Charles was through his life with the Amanab people. They turned their wailing into singing, proclaiming their belief in eternal life. In the name of Jesus Christ we pray. Amen.

90

Lean on a Solid Foundation

God's solid foundation stands firm.

2 TIMOTHY 2:19

For Mother's Day, 2004, I published a devotional book for my church called, *Her Children Call Her Blessed: Meditations on Mothers*. I mailed a copy to a woman named Kathy, whose story was in it. In 1999, her only child, David, died suddenly at the age of twenty-eight.

I had not heard from Kathy since her story was published in the newspaper in 2000. She sent me a thank you note for the book with the following update on her life:

> There have been many, many changes during the five years since David went "home." We were committed Christians before this happened, but David's death still brought indescribable anguish. Ultimately, however, it also brought a renewed commitment to the Lord. As a result of David's death, my husband and I were drawn into prison ministry. We now have seventy-five precious sons! We are now ordained prison ministers, and my husband has started attending seminary!"
> We have classes and services three days a week at the prison. We have been blessed again and again by these men. It is a maximum-security prison and 95 percent of our guys are there for life (most for murder). But now they are new men in Christ.

They are freer than many people on the "outside!"

Isn't it amazing how God has used these grieving parents in such a powerful way? What gave them the spiritual strength to respond to that tragedy the way they did?

Perhaps part of the answer is in a book God put in my hands at the time I asked that question. It's titled *Noah Built His Ark in the Sunshine* by James Moore. Noah prepared in advance for the storm that was to come. He used those bright days to build up the resources he would need when the dark floodwaters came.

As an example, the author told the story of a woman he visited who had just lost her husband in a sudden and tragic way. He said he was touched by her spirit of faith and thanksgiving. She said,

> Throughout the years I've heard many sermons on suffering and been in on many Sunday school discussions on sorrow. Those experiences at the church are helping me now. I am not blaming God. In fact, I know God is with me now as never before. I can feel his presence and strength. I am very grateful to the church for preparing me for this hour, and to God for being with me in it.[1]

You cannot borrow spiritual strength, and you cannot borrow someone else's faith when the tough times come. If you build a foundation over time, that foundation will support you and determine your reaction during times of crisis.

> *Dear Heavenly Father, Kathy and her husband suffered "indescribable anguish" when David died, but eventually they returned to the grace and love that you offer all of us when we are hurting. Thank you for their powerful witness to hurting souls. Help us to be diligent about building a foundation of faith that we can stand on when the floodwaters come. In the name of Jesus Christ we pray. Amen.*

---

1. Moore, James W. *Noah Built His Ark in the Sunshine* (Nashville: Dimensions for Living, 2003), 11-12.

91

Give Your Grief to the Lord

> *"Come to me, all you who are weary and burdened, and I will give you rest."*
>
> MATTHEW 11:28

Joni's mother struggled with lupus for many years. She was diagnosed in 1978 and was told she probably had around five years to live. But she decided five years was not enough and fought hard to live. She went through many surgeries, hospital stays, and various medications, many of which made her even sicker as her body rejected them.

Nine years after she was diagnosed, she was in intensive care for two months. The doctors didn't think she would make it. Joni said, "It was Christmas night in 1987 around midnight when my minister came up to sit with me in the waiting room. He told me that I needed to pray for God's will to be done. I remember thinking: *I will not pray for God's will if it is to take my mother!* I was pregnant with my second child and didn't want to lose Mom.

"Miraculously, Mom pulled through. She had a very strong faith and always believed the Lord was with her helping her through everything. She ended up in a wheelchair but always told me to remember when she was gone that she would be running through the streets of heaven and that when we met again, she would be standing to give me a hug!

"My heart was broken on June 14, 2002, when she left this world. We had been extremely close. I couldn't imagine living without her. I thought of all the things I would never enjoy again. One of the silliest was grape Popsicles. Mom loved Popsicles, but only the orange and red ones. She didn't like the grape. Whenever I visited, she made me eat the grape ones because she didn't want to waste them. Many days we sat in her living room talking and eating Popsicles.

"There are still many days that I am sad because I have to live my life without her. One day at work, I was thinking of a song that says, 'When you come to the place where I'm all you have, you'll find I'm all you need.'

"Mom had been gone for three years when I decided I was tired of carrying the pain and prayed, 'Jesus, today I'm giving it to you.'

"The Lord reminded me of the many years he gave us with Mom. She lived twenty-four years after the diagnosis, a miracle considering she was told she had five years to live. God showed me many other things to be thankful for: She got to see her grandkids grow up. My dad and I became closer. I was continually surrounded by a supportive husband, kids, and friends. I also thought about how my dad loved and cared for my mother all those years and was truly devoted to her. I thanked the Lord for the wonderful example he placed in my heart and in the hearts of the grandchildren.

"As I left work that day and started home, I felt a sense of peace. In fact, I stopped by the store and bought a box of Popsicles. I think tonight I'm ready to eat a grape one!"

God had been patiently waiting for Joni to hand him the burden.

Dear Heavenly Father, you promise that if we give you our burdens, you will give us rest for our souls. Help us to claim that promise. In the name of Jesus Christ we pray. Amen.

92

Ask for a Double Portion

"Let me inherit a double portion of your spirit."

2 KINGS 2:9

SUBJECT: One year ago today

That was the subject line in an e-mail message from a grieving relative named Bobbie. She wrote, "Today commemorates the one-year anniversary of my mother's passing, and tomorrow will be one month since my Dad died. I have received wonderful cards and letters of sympathy, but one piece of advice stood out to me and I thought I would share it with you."

Bobbie's friend wrote about a Bible story in 2 Kings and the remarkable lives of Elijah and Elisha, the most famous and dramatic of Israel's prophets. God appeared to Elijah and commanded him to anoint Elisha to succeed him as prophet. Elisha answered the call and became Elijah's attendant as they traveled together.

When Elijah's death was imminent, he asked Elisha, "What can I do for you before I am taken to heaven?" Elisha replied, "Let me inherit a double portion of your spirit." (2 Kings 2:9)

"When a dear one has died," wrote Bobbie's friend, "I think about one attribute that I most admired in that person. If that characteristic was gentleness, I'm aware that a certain amount of gentleness has gone out of the world, and if the world is not to be poorer, somebody must replace it. I then ask the Lord to give me a double portion of that lovely quality. From day to day I try very hard to live more gently, and often I find myself so caught up in the challenge that there is very little time to grieve."

Bobbie wrote of her friend's advice: "That sounds good to me, so I have asked God for a double portion of my parents' spirit of gentleness be upon me. In walking this road of grief and growth, I am challenged daily to dress in gentleness, a virtue hard to find in a society that admires toughness and roughness. We are encouraged to get things done and to get them done fast, even when people may get hurt in the process. Success, accomplishment, and productivity count, but the cost is high. There seems to be no place for gentleness in such a milieu.

"Matthew 12:20 says, 'Gentle is the one who does not break the crushed reed, or snuff the faltering wick.' Gentle is the one who is attentive to the strengths and weaknesses of the other and enjoys being together more than accomplishing something. A gentle person treads lightly, listens carefully, looks tenderly, and touches reverently. A gentle person knows that true growth requires nurture, not force. I want to dress myself with gentleness in our tough and often unbending world. Gentleness can be a vivid reminder of the presence of God among us."

Bobbie concluded her message with this challenge: "May we all be dressed in gentleness as we walk the road before us."

Dear Heavenly Father, what a wonderful way to honor a loved one: Ask for a double portion of the attribute you admired most in that person. Thank you for Bobbie's desire to carry on the spirit of gentleness that her mother and father exhibited. In the name of Jesus Christ we pray. Amen.

93

With God's Help You Can Go On

"And God will wipe away every tear from their eyes."
REVELATION 7:17

I was going through a file of story ideas when God showed me a two-year-old e-mail message from a friend named Marj. Her daughter, Elaine, had died two weeks earlier after a long battle with cancer. She was forty-eight years old, and left a husband and thirteen-year-old son.

I wrote Marj, asking how she was coping. She wrote:

> It has been two weeks since Elaine died. I do an awful lot of crying these days. It's hard for me to be with people right now, so please pray for me in that area. I want to smile and laugh again in recalling the many wonderful memories I have of her. I have always felt so fortunate that God gave Elaine to me. I guess I just didn't stop to think that he may have only loaned her to me for a while. I also am blessed each day as friends pay a visit to lift me up or when I receive my mail and find a note of encouragement. Yesterday I received a card from a friend, who enclosed this poem called 'You Can Go On' (author unknown):

You can shed tears because they're gone,
Or you can smile because they've lived.

You can close your eyes and pray they'll come back,
Or you can open your eyes and see all they've shared.

You can turn your back on tomorrow and live for yesterday,
Or you can be happy for tomorrow because of yesterday.

You can remember them and only that they've gone,
Or you can cherish their memory and let it live on.

You can cry and close your mind, be empty and turn your back,
Or you can do what they'd want: Smile, open your eyes, love, and go on.

When I read that poem, I felt as if Elaine were speaking to me. I know this is what our precious Jesus Christ wants for me and I am going to try to do it. I pray for God's grace to be sufficient each day to get me through that one twenty-four-hour period.

As I read Marj's two-year-old message, I wondered how she was doing now. I called her to see.

"Thank you for thinking of me," said Marj. "It has been a little over two years now since Elaine died. The bad days come less frequently now. I am able to remember the good things more and more. I still have days where the sadness comes in, because I'm reminded of Elaine by little things around me or something is said that triggers a memory. But the biggest change is that now I really feel blessed for having had her. I realize that none of us knows what our life span is here on earth. I believe God gave her to me because she was going to touch people. By being her mother, I was being blessed. I run into people all the time who tell me how Elaine touched their lives. That reaffirms to me that Elaine's life was short by our measurements, but it was full by God's measure. He used that short life for great things."

As parents, we tend to think we were put on this earth solely to parent our children, but God puts us here for other purposes too. One of those purposes may be that God uses us to show others that he will not desert us, even in the most trying times.

The death of a child must be one of the most painful things we can suffer on this earth. Contrary to popular belief, time does not heal all wounds. But the pain somehow becomes easier to bear when you can look back and remember the tender moments. God can help us do that.

Dear Heavenly Father, thank you for Marj's testimony about how God is working through her grief. Use her story as a comfort to others, that you can grow through the grief process. In the name of Jesus Christ we pray. Amen.

94

Unexpected Signs of Life

*He shall cover you with his feathers,
and under his wings you shall take refuge.*

PSALM 91:4

In my devotions one morning, God led me to read Psalm 91 titled, "Safety of Abiding in the Presence of God." It's one of my favorite Bible passages because it creates beautiful word pictures, especially verse 4: "He shall cover you with his feathers, and under his wings you shall take refuge."

When I read that verse, the Holy Spirit brought a powerful image to my mind that I saw years ago in a magazine: a full-page picture of the charred landscape after a forest fire. As far as the eye could see, it was black and lifeless.

The photographer was in search of the perfect picture to capture the feeling of complete devastation. He walked through an area that only a day before had been lush and green, teeming with all kinds of wildlife. He came upon a dead bird that he brushed with his foot as he walked by, and out from under the wings of that bird scampered three chicks! That photographer snapped a picture that brought new meaning to Psalm 91:4: "He shall cover you with his feathers, and under his wings you shall take refuge."

That mother bird gave her life so that her chicks could have life! Doesn't this remind you of someone else who gave his life so that we might live?

The Holy Spirit brought to mind another powerful lesson. Have you ever been in a situation where everything around you looked black and lifeless? Perhaps you were devastated at the loss of a loved one. Everything is lush and green one minute, and then the landscape of your life changes forever.

Sometimes we are so devastated that we can't see God or feel his presence as we walk through that valley. All we can do is put one foot in front of the other. But God promises he will walk with us through the fire.

It may be weeks or months later, but we will begin to see unexpected signs of life. After a forest fire, shoots of green grass and wild flowers eventually poke their heads through the blackened earth. New life bursts forth where we least expect it.

The same thing can happen after a crushing personal loss. We will see signs of life where we thought none existed.

Dear Heavenly Father, we can be secure under your protective wings as the fire rains down on us and our world falls apart. After the fire passes, open our eyes to signs of new life. Thank you that you always walk with us through the valleys, and thank you for Jesus who gave his life so that we might live forever. Amen.

SECTION FIFTEEN

JOY IN THE MIDST OF GRIEF

95

Can You Choose to Be Joyful?

Rejoice that your names are written in heaven.

LUKE 10:20

"Is it possible for people to choose joy in the midst of terrible circumstances?" I asked my pastor.

"Absolutely," said Pastor Jean. "The operative word here is 'choose.'"

She told the story of two young people, Tim and Sarah, both in their mid-20s. They were engaged to be married when they were involved in a horrific traffic accident. Sarah died at the scene. Tim was Life Lined to a hospital with massive head injuries. The family was called together, and they were told from the beginning that Tim would not live. A nurse approached the family and asked, "Would you like to be with him as he dies?"

"Yes," answered his mother. Tim was the youngest of four children. All the kids were there to say goodbye to him. They were a family of great faith and knew without a doubt that Tim would be in heaven with Jesus.

Pastor Jean said, "I stood with the mother and physically held her up as her legs wouldn't hold her. We held hands around Tim's bed as he quietly quit breathing."

Then his mother said, "Let's rejoice for Tim that he is in heaven with Jesus."

She softly began singing a lullaby that she sang to Tim when he was a baby. At the end of that lullaby the mother said, "Now, we can grieve."

Tim's mother was the perfect example of joy in the midst of grief: Rejoice first that he is in the arms of Jesus. And then grieve.

Dear Heavenly Father, thank you for this believer who chose to rejoice in one of life's most painful moments. We grieve because we are human. We rejoice because we know we have eternal life. In the name of your son Jesus Christ we pray. Amen.

96

The Gift of Baby Andrew

Weeping may last for the night, but joy comes in the morning.

PSALM 30:5

It was summertime as Sally prepared for the birth of her first baby. She said, "I don't think there ever was a more excited mom-to-be. We decorated the baby's room. We knew from ultrasounds that it would be a boy, so I had cute little boy outfits hanging in the closet."

At 1 AM on June 18, a very special baby named Andrew was born. He was a beautiful baby, with golden curls and bright blue eyes, but there was no celebrating in the delivery room. Sally said, "The doctor knew immediately there was something terribly wrong. They whisked him away for tests. A few hours later, we got the devastating news that our beautiful baby boy was born with only brain stem function. Only his heart and lungs were functioning. Andrew could not see, could not hear, and had frequent seizures."

Sally, the excited new mom, found herself taking an unexpected journey. She said, "My baby would never recognize me, would never look into my eyes, or say Mama. He was destined to spend his life in a coma-like state. We spent the first few weeks in the neonatal unit at the hospital, but eventually Andrew had to be transferred to a skilled nursing facility. He required around-the-clock care that we couldn't provide."

Joy in the Midst of Grief

Sally and her husband prayed continually for Andrew to go and be with Jesus. During the next few months, they were called eleven times to come as fast as they could because the end was near. Then his condition improved and the journey went on.

"After seventeen months of struggling to live, my sweet baby Andrew went to be with Jesus. He died on November 11: Veterans' Day. How appropriate. He was a veteran, a soldier, who fought his entire life.

"This seems like a sad story, but I consider it a privilege to have been Andrew's mom. He taught me about the kind of love God has for us—unconditional love. He couldn't talk, smile, or communicate, but when you held him, you sensed he was special, that you were sitting with the angels. I believe Andrew's short seventeen months here on earth were part of a bigger plan, a mission that God used to reach out and touch lives.

"One of the ladies who did the laundry for all the patients at Andrew's nursing home once shared with me that when she was having a bad day and her life was full of chaos, she would go into Andrew's room and hold him. She said she could almost see his halo, and she always sensed a peace that helped her with whatever problems she had.

"You see, he was, indeed, a special child with a special purpose. Maybe my son touched lives in other ways I am not even aware of, but one thing I know for certain: Andrew was and is a child of God. His short life on earth gave and continues to give glory to Jesus Christ our Lord, as I have been privileged to share my faith with others.

"This June 18, would have been Andrew's eighteenth birthday. I can talk about him now with joy. Jesus took away the pain and hurt. I know Andrew has a healthy body now and is in the arms of Jesus. What more could a parent want for their child?"

Sally ended her story by quoting her favorite verse, Psalm 30:5, "Weeping may last for the night, but joy comes in the morning."

> *Dear Heavenly Father, thank you for Andrew's life, for every life, no matter how short, serves a purpose. And thank you for Sally's willingness to share her testimony about God's love and care throughout her journey, a journey that ended with joy. In the name of Jesus Christ we pray. Amen.*

97

A Time to Be Born and a Time to Die

There is a time for everything, and a season for every activity under heaven: a time to be born and a time to die.

ECCLESIASTES 3:1-2

It was around 7 AM on Sunday, September 1, 2002. Connie was prepared to go to the hospital to witness a medical miracle—the birth of a grandson. While all babies are miracles, this one was unique because he was being born to her daughter-in-law who had leukemia when she was two years old. Doctors had told her that the chemotherapy and other treatments she had as a child would leave her unable to bear children.

Due to complications in the pregnancy, the doctor was going to induce labor at 8 AM. Just as Connie prepared to leave her house around 7:30, the telephone rang. It was her mother. "Somebody has to help your dad," she said. "I don't know what's wrong with him, but he's out of his mind in pain."

"My brother-in-law is an EMT, so I told Mother to call him right away," said Connie.

They took him by car to the emergency room where the doctors soon determined that he was dying from a rare form of leukemia.

They gave him only hours to live. He was moved to a hospice room so the family could be with him."

That was the beginning of the most traumatic day of Connie's life, a combination of intense joy and intense grief. On the second floor of the hospital, her dad was dying, and on the fifth floor, her daughter-in-law was in labor. Connie spent the day going back and forth between their rooms.

"At one point, I was so exhausted that when I got in the elevator, I couldn't remember what button to push. I didn't know if I was going up or down.

"At 10:30 that night, Daddy was in very bad shape. They didn't think he would live another ten minutes. Upstairs in the OB ward at exactly 10:30 my new grandbaby was born: a healthy 10-pound, 5-ounce boy, the first grandson in the family."

But Connie's dad didn't die Sunday night as the doctors predicted. In fact, he hung on for another three days. Connie said, "I spent time in Daddy's room, but then I went upstairs and held that new baby, full of promise and new life, like the calm in the midst of a storm. My son and his wife took their new baby home on Wednesday afternoon. Daddy died a few hours later on Wednesday night. They both went home on the same day—one to his earthly home, the other to his heavenly home."

Dear Heavenly Father, the cycle of life continues—new babies are born, while earthly lives come to an end. Thank you for the miracle of new life and for the miracle of eternal life with you, each in its own time, each bringing its own sense of joy. In the name of Jesus Christ we pray. Amen.

98

The Heroes of the Faith among Us

All these people were still living by faith when they died.

HEBREWS 11:13

"Why don't you come have lunch with me?" asked Mary. "I want to show you the five paintings I did for the art show."

Mary was a remarkable lady who lived at a local retirement home. She was still an accomplished artist, no small feat at the age of ninety-seven. Her paintings, as always, were amazing. I marveled at her ability to create such work at her age and with such a steady hand.

Mary responded, "I don't do it by myself. The Holy Spirit helps me. I always pray for guidance and a steady hand when I'm painting."

She was in good humor and full of life that day, which turned out to be our last visit. Mary passed away in her sleep two weeks later.

Sometimes we don't think about how much influence a person has on our life until they are gone. That is the case with Mary. Fifteen years ago, I gave my testimony at church about how I came to Christ. Mary wrote me a note that said, "Thank you for your testimony this morning. It's so wonderful to be able to see God working in our lives. The Bible study book *Experiencing God*[1] by Blackaby made me more aware of this."

I didn't know Mary very well at that time, but God used her in a powerful way by recommending that book. *Experiencing God* changed my life. Halfway through that study, God led me to quit my teaching job to do Christian writing and speaking full-time. Mary and I were fast friends after that and often talked about spiritual matters.

The day after Mary died, I talked to a friend named Sharon, who was also influenced by her life. "She was a prayer warrior," said Sharon. "People probably have no idea that twice a day she prayed for our whole city."

As Sharon thought about the sequence of events the day Mary died, she saw God's hand in it. She said, "I was awake, unable to sleep, between 4 and 5 AM. I thought about Mary. She had asked me to bring her a current copy of the *Upper Room Daily Devotional Guide*, so I made a mental note to drop off a copy to her on my way to work.

"I knocked on her door the next morning. No answer. So I stuck the devotional book inside the wreath on her door and headed on to work. I hadn't been there very long before I got a phone call that Mary died in her sleep that morning at 4:49 AM, during that time when I was awake thinking about her. When I heard the news of her death, I was upset for about an hour, but then I experienced great joy. I knew she was in heaven with Jesus.

"I experienced even greater joy when I turned to the lesson for that day, November 1, in *The Upper Room*. At the top of the page next to the date was a notation that it was 'All Saints Day,' a day in the Christian calendar when we remember the heroes of the faith. The lesson was titled 'Grandma's Faith.'" As I read the words, I substituted Mary's name in it. God arranged that lesson to coincide with Mary's homecoming. It said:

> The pastor began to speak eloquently of the person known simply as "Grandma".... The pastor began to elaborate on how much Grandma loved and prayed for everyone in her small town. He said, "If she knew you, odds are you were prayed for. ... Like the great heroes of the faith in Hebrews 11, Grandma simply did what she knew best by praying for and showing love to everyone she met.... Often we forget that the biblical heroes of faith were just ordinary people like you and me.[2]

Sharon said, "At the bottom of the page were these words: 'Prayer Focus: The Saints who have influenced me.' Without a doubt, Mary influenced my life. She was a hero of the faith."

This story appeared in the newspaper the day before Mary's funeral. Her family asked me to read it at her funeral. Only then did I learn from her daughter that Mary always wanted to die on November 1, All Saints Day. God arranged that!

Dear Heavenly Father, yes, the heroes of the faith in Hebrews 11 were just ordinary people, but what made them extraordinary was their total reliance on you. Thank you so much for Mary's life and her love for you. Amidst our grief, we celebrate with joy her homecoming with you in heaven. In the name of Jesus Christ we pray. Amen.

---

1. Blackaby, Henry T. and Claude V. King. *Experiencing God: Knowing and Doing the Will of God* (Nashville: LifeWay Press, 1990).

2. *Upper Room Daily Devotional Guide* (Nashville: The Upper Room), Nov. 1, 2005.

99

Because He Lives

Because I live, you also will live.

JOHN 14:19

Steve and Vicki decided to celebrate their thirty-fifth wedding anniversary with a one-week Gaither cruise, hosted by Bill and Gloria Gaither, well-known names in the Christian music industry.

Vicki said, "It was one of the most amazing experiences I have ever had: 1,800 Christians gathered to praise the Lord. We were from all different denominations and walks of life, but we were bound together as brothers and sisters in Christ."

Vicki and Steve attended concerts every night. A phenomenal pianist named Anthony Burger was one of the big draws. He is well known in the gospel music circle. In fact, he has played at Carnegie Hall and has entertained presidents. He is one of those rare performers who is known simply by his first name, Anthony.

"Anthony had an amazing faith story," said Vicki. "When he was a toddler, he tipped over his baby walker and fell onto a red-hot floor furnace. He had severe burns on his face, hands and legs. In fact, his hands were so badly burned that doctors said he would never be able to use his hands. Not only was Anthony able to use his hands, but God gave him an incredible talent that he chose to use for God's glory.

There were two concerts each night. Vicki and Steve always attended the early concert and then ate dinner afterward. Halfway through the cruise they walked out of the dining room as usual. They noticed several ladies crying, so they asked what was wrong.

"Pray for Anthony and his family. He just collapsed and died right in the middle of the concert."

Vicki and Steve were stunned. They had heard him play one hour earlier. Anthony was only forty-four years old. His wife and twelve-year-old daughter were also on the cruise.

"We thought this would ruin the rest of the cruise," said Vicki. "But the next morning, at the time when Anthony would have performed again, Bill Gaither came out on stage and talked about Anthony's amazing life and how God used his life so powerfully. It turned into a joyful celebration of his life."

"Anthony died doing what he loved," Bill began, "praising the Lord through his gift of music. Even as he was going down, he was reaching for the piano keys. What a blessing to be used by God until your last breath!"

Vicki said, "We walked into that auditorium devastated and walked out full of joy and praise to God for this man's life. I underestimated the power of God to use this for his glory. The entire tone of the cruise changed in a good way. Before, it was very upbeat and uplifting, but after his death, everyone was so humbled before the Lord. We felt the power of the Holy Spirit as never before speaking to our hearts. This man won many awards, including 'Best Instrumentalist in Gospel Music,' but those worldly awards meant nothing as he ran into the arms of his Father."

At the end of the cruise, Anthony's wife and daughter joined the Gaithers on stage. The last song they sang was "Because He Lives," one of the Gaither's signature tunes.

Vicki said, "I have sung that song a hundred times. It's easy to sing it when things are fine in your life, but when you sing it as you are going through bad times and really listen to the words, it's life changing."

In John 14:9, Jesus comforts his disciples as he prepares to leave them. He taught, "Because I live, you also will live."

JOY IN THE MIDST OF GRIEF

In John 16:20-22, Jesus continues his teaching with these words: "You will grieve, but your grief will turn to joy. . . . I will see you again and you will rejoice, and no one will take away your joy."

Dear Jesus, thank you that you gave us the kind of joy that no one can take away from us, the joy that comes from knowing you as our personal Lord and Savior. It is in your name we pray. Amen.

100

Turn to Him and Embrace the Promise

"For God so loved the world that he gave his one and only Son, that whoever believes in him shall not perish but have eternal life."

JOHN 3:16

When a young, single mother with a small child died suddenly in a car accident, my Pastor Jean was called to talk with her grieving co-workers. What words of comfort can be spoken at a time like that?

She began: "It is right that we should gather here as we grieve the loss of our friend and co-worker. My dear mother used to say: 'When a baby is born, we rejoice and the baby cries. When a friend or loved one dies, they rejoice and we cry.'

"We cry for many reasons. We didn't get a chance to say goodbye. She was at the next desk or in the next office yesterday and now she's gone. We cry for her little daughter who lost her mother. We cry because we think she died too young. The list can go on and on.

"But as Christians we also have reason to rejoice. I like to use the seashell analogy," continued Pastor Jean, as she held up a seashell for everyone to see. "There used to be a little critter living in this shell. I believe that's what happens when we die. The person in that shell of a body is no longer there. My faith tells me she is in heaven with God. That's the promise I hold on to."

Jesus promised in John 3:16, "Whoever believes in him shall not perish but have eternal life."

Turn to him and embrace that promise.

> *Dear Heavenly Father, Thank you for the promise that we will live in eternal life with you when we acknowledge your son Jesus Christ as our Lord and Savior. It is in his holy name that we pray. Amen.*

101

Such a Simple Message: Choose Joy

> *Rejoice always*
>
> 1 THESSALONIANS 5:16

On my desk, I have a framed copy of four translations of 1 Thessalonians 5:16:

"Rejoice always." (RSV)

"Be joyful always." (NIV)

"Rejoice evermore." (KJV)

"Choose joy." (Wes Nash)

That last translation is by a man named Wes Nash, who died after a two-year battle with cancer. When he was first diagnosed, he was given two months to live. Wes, through his faith-filled life, turned that two months into two years.

When Wes and his wife, Patty, first learned of the diagnosis, they had a good cry. But then Wes went to another room to pray and read his Bible. That's when he came across the verse 1 Thessalonians. 5:16, "Be joyful always." When he came out of the room, he was literally glowing and said, "I choose joy."

Patty laughed and said, "I always thought Wes had a glow about him! Yes, he chose Joy with a capital J, and he always gave Jesus the credit."

"We prayed everyday that God would use us through the battle to witness to others. Wes felt it was an honor to be used by God. He understood that this was not an earthly battle, but a spiritual battle. We're all dying, but the physical body has very little to do with it. Wes' philosophy was that if you give in to sorrow and defeat, then you are letting Satan win. He said, 'I choose to keep my eyes on Jesus. I choose joy.'"

Another friend said to me, "Wes was such a blessing to the people around him."

"Yes," I answered. "How many people choose joy when they're dying?"

She countered with: "How many people choose joy when they're living?"

As I wrote this story, my husband was reading a book called *Life Is an Attitude,* by Dottie Billington. Chapter 19 is titled, "You Can Choose How to React." The crux of the chapter is this: You can let a bad situation overwhelm you and embitter you, or you can choose to have a positive attitude. You can decide to let the challenges in your life get the better of you, or you can use them as stepping stones toward growth. The only thing you have control over is your response.[1]

How do you respond to life's challenges? Only faith in Jesus Christ results in perfect joy and peace through the power of the Holy Spirit. Choose joy.

> *Dear Heavenly Father, thank you for reminding us through Wes that we can choose joy in any and all circumstances through the power of the Holy Spirit. In the name of Jesus Christ we pray.*
> *Amen.*

---

1. Billington, Dottie. *Life Is an Attitude: How to Grow Forever Better* (Sammamish: Lowell Leigh Books, 2001), 95-97.

BIBLIOGRAPHY

Alpha Course, London: Alpha International. 1995.

Blackaby, Henry T. and Claude V. King. *Experiencing God: Knowing and Doing the Will of God*. Nashville: LifeWay Press, 1990.

Blackaby, Henry, *The Experience: Day by Day with God*. Nashville: Broadman & Holman Publishers, 1999.

Billington, Dottie. *Life Is an Attitude: How to Grow Forever Better.* Sammamish: Lowell Leigh Books, 2001.

Callanan, Maggie and Patricia Kelley. *Final Gifts: Understanding the Special Awareness, Needs and Communications of the Dying*. New York: Bantam Books, 1997.

Graham, Billy. *Angels: God's Secret Agents*. Nashville: W. Publishing Group, 1994.

Graham, Billy. *The Indianapolis Star*, "We Were Not Created for This Life Alone." May 31, 2008.

Gumbel, Nicky. *Questions of Life: A Practical Introduction to the Christian Faith*. Colorado Springs: Cook Communications Ministries, 1993.

Hayford, Jack W. *Spirit Filled Life Bible NKJV*. Nashville: Thomas Nelson Publishers, 1991.

Kalas, J. Ellsworth. *The Grand Sweep.* Nashville: Abington Press, 1996.

Kelly, Cliff Ph.D., entry on website: http//www.bethanylutheran.org/brimemories.html, Jan. 5, 2006.

Life Application Study Bible, NIV. Grand Rapids: Zondervan Publishing House, 1991.

Moore, James W. *Noah Built His Ark in the Sunshine*. Nashville: Dimensions for Living, 2003.

Marshall, Catherine. *Moments That Matter: Inspiration for Each Day of the Year*. Nashville: Countryman, a Division of Thomas Nelson, Inc., 2001.

Rogers, Roberta. *Is That You, Lord?* Grand Rapids: Chosen Books, 2000.

Roth, Ron. *Holy Spirit: The Boundless Energy of God*. Carlsbad: Hay House, Inc., 2000.

Russell, A. J. *God Calling*. Uhrichsville: Barbour and Company, Inc., 1989.

Serendipity Bible, 10th Anniversary Edition, NIV. Grand Rapids: Zondervan Publishing House and Serendipity House, 1988.

Ten Boom, Corrie. *The Hiding Place*. Grand Rapids: Chosen Books, 1971.

Williams, Charles, Rev. *The Indianapolis Star*, "Treating This Holiday As If It Were Your Last." Dec. 26, 2006.

Wogelmuth, Dan, President, Youth for Christ World Outreach, entry on website: http//www.bethanylutheran.org/brimemories.html, Dec. 16, 2005.

Wright, Norman. *The Victory: Overcoming the Trials of Life*. Richardson: Grace Products Corporation, 2000.

Upper Room Daily Devotional Guide. Nashville: The Upper Room, Nov. 1, 2005.

Zacharias, Ravi. *Recapture the Wonder*. Nashville: Thomas Nelson, Inc., 2003.

ALSO AVAILABLE:

> The *Companion Guide for God in the Midst of Grief:*
> *101 True Stories of Comfort*

A valuable resource for:

- Individuals who want to reflect more deeply on the stories in the book, *God in the Midst of Grief: 101 True Stories of Comfort.*

- Those who want space for personal journaling.

- Leaders of seminars, retreats, or workshops on death and dying.

- Small group leaders who want thought-provoking questions to enhance group discussions, as in:

    ❖ Adult Sunday school classes;
    ❖ Small group studies;
    ❖ Grief support groups;
    ❖ Book discussion groups.

- Includes a "Topical Index" for group leaders to quickly reference a topic on grief when the need arises.

Contact Diane Pearson for more information.

dipearson@comcast.net

www.dianepearson.org